ANCIENT TAMIL NADU
GLIMPSES OF THE PAST

by K. Indrapala

This International Edition Published 2021 by Ohm Books Publishing, UK.

www.ohmbooks.com

ISBN: 9798590567386

TO

THE YOUTH OF TAMIL NADU

AND TO

The Late Lamented Scholar and Good Friend
Padma Shri Prof. Noboru Karashima
who devoted his life to the study of ancient Tamil inscriptions
and provided fresh interpretations to the
medieval history of Tamil Nadu

Preface

This book is written for the benefit of young readers in Tamil Nadu. This state has a long history and a rich heritage. Its history is full of remarkable achievements in various fields. It has impressive archaeological remains dating back to the early centuries of the Common Era (CE). What is more interesting is that there are thousands of stone inscriptions, some of which go back to the second century Before the Common Era (BCE). In addition, a large number of magnificent temples have survived bearing testimony to the achievements of the ancients in art and architecture. The past is fascinating and an enduring source of inspiration.

Today breathtaking developments are taking place in science and technology. These can be used to discover more of the past and understand it better. Much remains to be discovered. It is important for the youth to know the past. This helps to understand the present. This book is intended to give a peep into that past.

K. Indrapala
14th January 2020

Contents

Map - 1: Ancient Tamilnadu

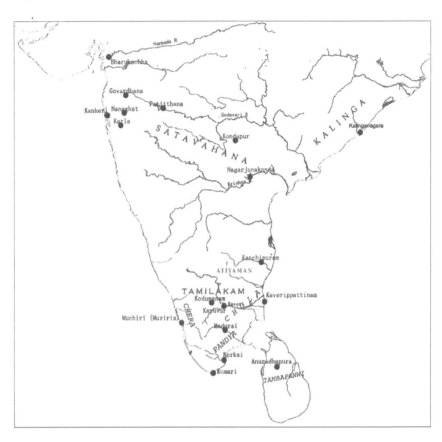

(After Y. Subbarayalu)

Section 1 *Ancestors*

1   Journey from Africa

All of this – all of us – began in equatorial Africa over a million years ago as Africans with black skins and the full suite of associated physical features. Neil Oliver, *A History of Ancient Britain* (London *2011).*

Every one of you, or almost everyone, would like to know who your ancestors were and where they came from. You have probably been told a story about the origins of your ancestors. You may have found that this story took you back into a mythical past. Or, you may have been told not an origin myth but about a claim that your people are among the oldest on the planet.

Origin myths

Origin myths are common in most societies. In the distant past many people had belief in these myths. But in this century the advance of scientific knowledge has forced all origin myths to lose their credibility, although the Internet enables many to peddle their myths to unsuspecting enthusiasts on a scale never seen before. As a result, many are confused. Young people like you are at a loss to know what to accept. It is therefore important for you to check who is telling you what.

Hominids

So, let us see what today's leading scientists are telling us about the human past. That is a good beginning. Much research is being done with the latest advanced techniques in some of the reputed universities, mainly in the Western countries, on the origin and spread of human beings. It is now widely agreed among scientists that the earliest humans were found in Africa. Before humans, for millions of years, there were other animals, both large and small. Then came the human types. They are called hominids. There were several species of these early humans. One of them was the Homo erectus (the upright man). Scientists believe that the Homo erectus had a body very much like modern humans. From Africa some of them moved to different parts of Asia, including China and Indonesia. Another hominid type, popularly known as Neanderthals, spread to West Asia and Europe.

Homo sapiens

About 200,000 years ago a new species of humans appeared in Africa. This one, known as the Homo sapiens, is considered to be the species from which all modern humans are descended.

With the emergence of this species the others became extinct. Some scientists believe that in some places the Homo sapiens interbred with some of the earlier humans, especially the Neanderthals. For the moment, we shall begin our story with the emergence of the Homo sapiens.

For more than a 100,000 years these modern type humans lived in Africa making very little progress. Already, before the emergence of Homo sapiens, the earlier humans had taken some important steps in the long human journey to conquer the world. More than a million years ago, early humans began to change their natural way of life. This helped to make them different from all the other animals.

One of the first steps they took to change their life was to use tools. These were mainly stones, sticks and bones found in the natural environment. There were other animals and birds, too, that used tools (and still do), like the chimpanzee, gorilla, raven and crow. But humans used stones and sticks far more effectively and in a wide variety of ways because of their very flexible fingers and arms. Having developed the ability to stand upright and walk on their two legs (bipedalism), they were able to free their hands to make and use better tools. Bipedalism was a major development in the human story. Soon they took the next important step – making tools to suit their needs. The Homo sapiens who came later kept improving these tools and there was no end to it, as we all know.

Hunter – gatherers

But progress was very slow. Homo sapiens lived as hunter-gatherers for more than 100,000 years. Hunter-gatherers were people who hunted small animals and gathered fruits, yams and other edible vegetables in their environment for their food. The earliest humans were mainly herbivores, that is, they ate vegetarian food. But gradually they began to eat meat, often from animal bodies left over by carnivores (meat-eating animals). They may also have eaten meat of animals burnt in bushfires. This would have been their first taste of cooked meat. Plant foods, however, formed their main diet. As they began to eat more and more meat, they also began to make better tools for hunting and cutting animal flesh.

Out of Africa

As the Homo sapiens improved their tools and created spears and arrows they moved long distances following their prey. As their prey moved with changing seasons, so did bands of these early humans. Some bands wandered across the eastern part of Africa. Some of them arrived at the north-eastern part of the African continent some 70,000 years ago.

While some details relating to this migration may be debated by scientists and may get revised as more research is done, there is general agreement that a particular group of Homo sapiens migrated out of Africa from the northeast region sometime between 85,000 and 65,000 years ago. Scientists also generally agree that it is from this group that all modern non- Africans are descended.

These modern humans moved along the coast of the Arabian peninsula and then along the Iranian coast to the western coast of the Indian peninsula (see Map 1). Moving down the coast some reached the southern part of the peninsula while some others moved inland. This southern part was much larger than the modern south India and included Sri Lanka, too.

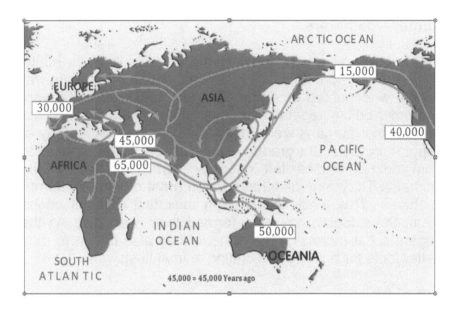

Map 2 - Migration out of Africa

Ages in Prehistory

Palaeolithic Age = Old Stone Age
Mesolithic Age = Middle Stone Age
Neolithic Age = New Stone Age

What is CE and BCE?

CE = Common Era (same as AD)
BCE = Before the Common Era (same as BC)

An example of a stone handaxe used by early humans in Africa

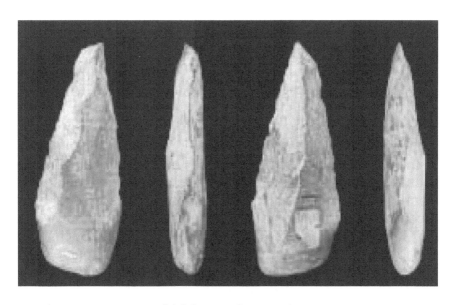

Old Stone Age tools

Section 1 *Ancestors*

2   Arrival of Homo Sapiens in Tamil Nadu

One day in the distant past, possibly more than 10,000 years after the first Homo sapiens left Africa, the first of their descendants set foot on the land forming the southern part of the Indian peninsula, the territory comprising the modern states of Kerala and Tamil Nadu. (The area of these two states roughly formed the ancient Tamilnadu about 2,500 years ago.) When this happened the total population of modern humans in the world was only about 10,000, according to scientists studying prehistoric migrations.

What do we know about these early ancestors? What was the environment like when they arrived here? What did they confront here? The answers to these questions can only be speculative, that is, we can only guess. The evidence we have about these early ancestors is still very little. But, with what has already been concluded by scientists, it is possible to give a general picture of these humans and the environment in which they found themselves.

Toba Volcano

At the time Homo sapiens came out of Africa, and for thousands of years after that, major changes in climate were deeply influencing every continent. There was also a huge volcanic eruption in Sumatra (Indonesia) about 73,500 years ago. It is known as the Toba volcanic eruption. Such huge eruptions are extremely rare and are known as supervolcanic eruptions. The Toba eruption resulted in a heavy cloud of ash covering a good part of Asia and cooling the earth considerably. The clouds of heated ash spewed out by the volcano spread more than 3,000 kilometres away. This ash has been found buried in India and the South China Sea.

Layers of this ash have been found in Jwalapuram (in Kurnool District, Andhra). There is no doubt that the area of Tamil Nadu was also much affected by the volcanic ash. It is believed that the heavy cloud of volcanic ash spewed out into the atmosphere blocked the sunlight for a long time causing an icy cold winter. It is also believed that a good part of the forests in India were destroyed by the Toba volcanic eruption.

A huge volcanic eruption, known as a supervolcanic eruption, occurred about 73, 500 years ago in the island of Sumatra (Indonesia) at the site of modern Lake Toba.

South India

By the time Homo sapiens appeared in south India the climate had changed considerably. Tropical forests, with lush green vegetation, would have been covering the whole region. Two of Tamil Nadu's favourite trees, the sandalwood and the cinchona (now endangered), no doubt flourished in these forests. The Asian elephant, Indian leopard, wild boar, sambur, mongoose, palm squirrel, porcupine and the pretty lion-tailed macque and possibly the Asian cheetah (now extinct in India) roamed freely in these forests. There were also colourful birds like the peafowl, jungle fowl, woodpecker and the wood pigeon. Prominent among the reptiles were the Indian cobra and the mugger crocodile. Into this noisy, colourful and salubrious environment walked in the Homo sapiens.

Homo erectus

It is not known whether any surviving members of the earlier human types, like the Homo erectus, were in Tamil Nadu when the first Homo sapiens arrived. There is evidence for the presence of Homo erectus in India before the Toba eruption. The skeletal remains of only one Homo erectus, named the Narmada Human, have been discovered in India but stone tools used by early human types have been found in several places. In Tamil Nadu, several very ancient stone tools have been found at Attirampakkam (60 km away from Chennai). However, it is possible that the impact of the Toba eruption might have led to the extinction of the Homo erectus in Tamil Nadu.

African features

Coming along a tropical route from north Africa to south Asia, the Homo sapiens who came to south India had black skin, curly hair and other physical features like their ancestors in Africa. For those who moved into the colder regions of Europe and Northeast Asia, the cold climate and other environmental factors brought about changes in the colour of their skin, eyes and hair. Those who made their home in India, Sri Lanka, Southeast Asia and Australia retained their dark skin colour and other African features for thousands of years.

Early skills

What skills did the Homo sapiens bring to south India? Long before Homo sapiens appeared in Africa, other human species who were their ancestors had acquired many skills that helped them to progress from the natural way of life that animals lead. The large size of their brain and the deftness of their fingers enabled them to make better and better tools to change their lives.

They made tools out of stone, bone, antler and wood. Sharp stone knives were made to cut meat and fruits. They used stone to grind nuts and process food (the stone mortar and pestle we use in our modern kitchens is a survival from this ancient past). They also learnt to shape organic material such as antler, bone and ivory into implements, like needles. They hunted small animals and caught fish and other marine creatures. They were able to pierce shells and carve bones and use them as jewellery. One of the most important skills they had was the ability to control fire. Fire, as you, know, is a bad master but a good servant. As long as they knew how to control it, they were able to use it to roast their meat, keep themselves warm and even defend themselves against big animals.

Homo sapiens brought all these skills with them when they came to south India. They did not settle in one place but kept moving with the animals they hunted. They also caught fish in the rivers. Food was always the driving force that kept them moving.

Sri Lanka

Some of them moved farther south into the land now known as Sri Lanka (it was not separated from south India until about 7,000 years ago). There, among the caves used by these early humans, archaeologists have found microlithic (small stone) tools, beads made of shells, bone points and some human remains. These are among the earliest modern human remains found in the whole of South Asia. They are dated to 26,500 BCE (that is, nearly 28,500 years ago). Remains of animals eaten by these humans as well as plant food have also been found in these caves. These include remains of pig, deer, squirrel and porcupine. The fruits include wild banana and breadfruit. The humans who used these caves had also brought marine shells from the coast.

Paleolithic Age

Until about 10,000 years ago these early humans lived in what archaeologists call the Palaeolithic (Old Stone) Age. Tools used in this period have been found in several places in Kerala and Tamil Nadu. Tenkara, Gudiyam, Vadamadurai and Attirampakkam are some of these places.

Mesolithic Age

The Palaeolithic Age was followed by the Mesolithic (Middle Stone) Age from about 4000 BCE. An important development in this period was the use of microliths or small stone blades. These were fitted on to long sticks or wooden handles to make arrows, spears and better knives. Many Mesolithic sites have been found in Kerala and Tamil Nadu. Tenmalai (Kerala) and the Pamban coast in the Tirunelveli District are well known sites. The Mesolithic Age lasted till about 1000 BCE.

Until the end of the Mesolithic Age no major developments took place. But some very important events were taking place in certain parts of the outside world. While the early humans were peacefully roaming about in south India with their stone age tools, climate change was affecting some other distant parts of the earth. From about 21,000 to 18,000 BCE, that is about 20,000 years ago, land temperatures fell drastically and northern Europe as well as North America were completely covered with ice. It was an Ice Age there. By the end of the Ice Age many large animals had become extinct. Elsewhere, in Africa and South America, deserts expanded. South India was not affected by these major changes.

Southwest Asia

Nearer home, in Southwest Asia (modern Iraq, Jordan, Syria, Turkey, Israel and Palestine) and in the northwestern part of the Indian subcontinent (the Indus Valley) as well as in East Asia humans were making great progress towards civilization. In Southwest Asia we see the domestication of certain plants and animals which soon led to the beginnings of farming. After several thousand years of life as hunter-gatherers, farming was a major revolution for humans. It led to settled life and the emergence of villages. Not long afterwards we see the rise of the first cities and the first civilizations in Iraq, Egypt and the Indus Valley (India- Pakistan).

Settled villages

With farming and herding of goats, sheep and cattle, villages were established. Some of these grew into the world's first towns. The world's oldest town that we know has been discovered in Turkey, in a place called Catalhöyük. Farmers and herders established a large settlement in the area which grew into a town of more than 3,000 people about 9,400 years ago. It had houses which were built close together. We also see here early signs of religious activity. The people here seem to have worshipped a mother goddess and paid respect to bulls. At about the same time another bigger town was built in Jericho in the Jordan Valley (in modern West Bank, Palestine). Some of the first steps towards civilization were taken in these early towns.

First cities

All these developments soon led to the rise of the first cities and civilization. This happened first in Mesopotamia (modern Iraq), then in the Nile Valley in Egypt. The first cities in the Indus Valley came soon afterwards. The rise of civilization in China was not far behind. In south India, however, until the beginning of the Iron Age about 3,000 years ago the people lived as hunter-gatherers uninfluenced by any of these developments. They continued to live in the Mesolithic or Middle Stone Age. As a new culture, with settled life in villages and an economy marked by cattle-keeping, began to spread in the northern regions of Tamil Nadu (Dharmapuri, Salem and North Arcot Districts) from Andhra and Karnataka, other new influences came from outside and changed the way of life of the people in Tamil Nadu.

What Have We Got from the People of Mesopotamia?

Apart from the wheel and the art of writing which the world has found extremely valuable ever since their invention, certain other aspects of the legacy (what they have given to us) of the Mesopotamian people (Babylonians) are always with us in this modern world, in fact in everyday use.

Do you know that almost every minute we are using something that the Babylonians invented? When we look at the time, when we refer to a day by name, when we count the weeks, we are using a method that these people gave us. Have you ever wondered why there are sixty minutes in an hour and not a convenient number like hundred? That is because the Babylonians counted in blocks of sixty – so we have sixty seconds in a minute and sixty minutes in an hour. This was their way of measuring time.

They also divided the circle into 360 parts or degrees. We have seven days in a week and not a convenient number like ten. Again, this is a system they had. Even some of the names of the days, like Sunday and Monday (that is, Day of the Sun and Day of the Moon) are names given by them.

The World Outside

While the people in south India were in the Middle Stone Age, many important developments took place in West Asia and certain other parts of the world. This is a brief list of some of these developments:

About 10000 BCE : Farming begins in West Asia

About 7000 BCE : The world's oldest towns, Catalhöyük and Jericho are flourishing

Excavated area at CatalhÖyuk

Jericho - Ruins of one of the oldest towns

About 5000 BCE : Farming begins in the Nile Valley

About 5000 BCE : Farming begins in China

About 3500 BCE : People in Mesopotamia (modern Iraq) build the world's first cities

About 3500 BCE : The wheel is invented in Mesopotamia

About 3200 BCE : Writing is invented in Mesopotamia

Mesopotamia : An artist's impression of the original city

About 3000 BCE : Beginning of the Indus Valley civilization

About 2700 BCE : Silk is first produced in China

About 2500 BCE : Egyptians start building the Great Pyramid at Giza

About 2000 BCE : Minoans build palaces in Crete (Greece, Europe)

About 1500 BCE : End of the Indus Valley civilization

About 1500 BCE : Arrival of Sanskrit-speakers in India

Section 2 *Early Iron Age*

1 The Arrival of Iron

About 3,000 years ago the people of south India began to feel the effects of some of the major developments that had taken place in the outside world. In the northwestern part of the Indian subcontinent, rising in the fertile valley of the mighty Indus River (the original Sanskrit form of this name was Sindhu), a great civilization had spread over a large part of modern Pakistan and northwest India. Its major cities, now known as Harappa and Mohenjodaro, were in Pakistan but there were many of their cities as far south as Gujarat.

The people of this civilization were very advanced. They built well planned cities with a surprising drainage system. Their traders went to distant places, including the West Asian cities in and around Mesopotamia. They used a writing system to help them in this trade. It is possible that their traders sailed down as far south as modern Tamil Nadu and Sri Lanka in search of such items as pearls, ivory and peacock feathers.

Sanskrit – speakers

But after the fall of the Indus Civilization traders did come to south India and Sri Lanka. The fall of the great cities of the Indus valley took place about 3,500 years ago. At that time, a new group of people speaking the Sanskrit language entered the Indus valley. They followed a religion dominated by an educated priestly class called Brahmins. Their religion and language were powerful forces that soon spread across north India and changed the course of history in South Asia.

Iron Age

Before these new forces spread to south India, another major development took place. This was the spread of an Iron Age culture that introduced the making of pottery, the use of iron and farming. The result was the beginning of settled life and the rise of villages. With such far-reaching developments, Tamil Nadu entered what may be called the Early Iron Age. This was about 1000 BCE, roughly 3,000 years ago.

This new culture introduced several important elements of civilization to south India. These include a basic iron-using technology, making of pottery with a potter's wheel, the use of a plough, the cultivation of rice, the building of small reservoirs and dams for irrigating fields, specialised crafts such as carpentry and the know-how to control the environment in a better way than before. All these led to the growth of villages and the development of trade. New burial practices were associated with the growth of rituals and religious observances. Settled life resulted in the emergence of chiefdoms. The horse was introduced at this time and this led to the growth of the power of chiefs and conflicts among them. Thus, in the Early Iron Age, between about 1000 BCE and 300 BCE, major changes took place in south India.

A potsherd with designs from the Early Iron Age site at Adichchanallur, Tamil Nadu

This new culture, which is also known as the megalithic culture, began to spread from western India (Maharashtra) about 1200 BCE. Its origin is not known. From the west, it spread to Karnataka and then into Andhra and Tamil Nadu as well as Kerala. This culture is associated with burials which are often grouped in clusters. Some of them have large stones over them and it is for this reason that the culture has acquired the name Megalithic (megalith = big stone). Some of the burials contain urns with skeletal remains or ashes collected after cremation. Different types of burials are found in different areas. The most famous Early Iron Age burial site is Adichchanallur.

Section 2 *Early Iron Age*

2   Traders, Brahmins and Monks

Of the many important developments that took place in the Early Iron Age, one that led to the spread of cultural influences from outside was the arrival of long-distance traders. These traders came by boat along the western coast as well as the eastern coast and overland across the Vindhya mountains. They came from north India and possibly from West Asia and the Indus Valley. Along with the traders came religious leaders who introduced new forms of worship and religious practices. Traders also seem to have introduced ideas about the art of writing and possibly also a language- related influence.

It is not easy to find out when traders from distant lands first came to the region that is now Tamil Nadu. Traders from the Indus Valley and West Asia, especially the Phoenicians, may have been among the earliest to come to the shores of south India. The narrow sea between Tamil Nadu and Sri Lanka (Gulf of Mannar) has been well known for thousands of years for its pearls and chanks (conch shells). It is possible that traders from the Indus Valley came to this area looking for pearls or conch shells. It is believed that the Phoenicians from the Mediterranean region came to the Gulf of Mannar to get pearls.

Pandya chiefdom

The arrival of long-distance traders seems to have led to the rise of an important chiefdom in the south coast. This was the chiefdom of the Pandyas in a place called Matirai (which later came to be known as Madurai). The visits of traders from far-off countries would have led to the emergence of an exchange centre and the rise to power of a local chief. Matirai appears to have been that exchange-centre. The Pandya clan of this place seems to have begun its rise to power with the arrival of long- distance traders. Possibly the chiefdom of the Pandyas was the first of its kind in ancient Tamil Nadu.

Burial urns from Adichchanallur

Several questions remain to be answered for us to know more about this chiefdom in the Early Iron Age. Some scholars have argued that the names of some of the items brought by traders from foreign lands to the kingdom of King Solomon in Israel about 3,000 years ago are mentioned in the Hebrew Bible with names derived from Tamil. Did Phoenician traders come to Tamil Nadu 3,000 years ago?

About the same time, the Sanskrit Vedas refer to pearls. Some Sanskrit books written after the Vedas mention pearls from the Pandya territory. Did trade with north India help the Pandyas to build a powerful chiefdom? Did traders from the Indus Valley visit the Pandya ports in the Early Iron Age? Did these visits lead to traders and others from the Indus cities settling in the Pandya territory when the decline of the Indus Civilization took place? Many people believe that the language of the Indus people is related to Tamil. Ancient traditions associate Madurai and the Pandyas with the Tamil language. The area ruled by the Pandyas appears to have been the home of Tamil in very ancient times.

Kaveripattinam

Another important port for traders coming from north India that rose to prominence in the Early Iron Age was Kaveripattinam. This may have helped the rise of a chiefdom controlled by the Cholas. On the west coast, trade with north India contributed to the rise of another important port called Musiri. The chiefdom of the Cheras benefited from the trade at this port.

Religious leaders

Traders carried tales about Tamil Nadu back to their homelands. Soon there were others travelling with them to the south. Among them were religious leaders, fortune-seekers and adventurers. Brahmins with their knowledge of the Vedas and Vedic rituals were among the earliest religious leaders to arrive. With the rise of new religions like Jainism, Buddhism and the Ajivika religion in north India, monks belonging to these religions came to the south to spread their beliefs. The arrival of Brahmin leaders and the manner in which they spread new influences in the south are preserved in many ancient legends. The most important of these legends are those about the sage Agastya and the Brahmin leader Parasurama.

Agastya

Agastya as represented in an Indonesian sculpture

There are many legends that tell about the arrival of Brahmins and others from north India. These are found in the Sanskrit epics *(Mahabharata and Ramayana)* and other Sanskrit books. Many temples in Kerala and Tamil Nadu also have their own legends. A central figure in some of these legends is the sage Agastya. These legends say that he crossed the Vindhya mountains, established his hermitage in the south, married a princess called Lopamudra and controlled the Rakshasas (demons) who gave trouble to him. He is credited with introducing literature to the south and writing the first grammar of the Tamil language.

Parasurama

Parasurama, as represented in a modern painting

The legends about Parasurama are associated with the coming of the Brahmins to Kerala. Parasurama was a Brahmin warrior who used a powerful axe *(parasu)*. He was responsible for settling Brahmins in Kerala which was a land that he created. He threw his divine axe across the sea from Gokarna (on the west coast). The axe fell in the region of Kanyakumari (Cape Comorin) and all the sea between Gokarna and Kanyakumari became dry land which Parasurama donated to the Brahmins.

Section 3 *Dawn of History*

1   Ashoka's Missions

History begins with written records.

Until about 2,300 years ago there were no written records telling us about what was happening in south India or about the people living there. In the reign of the Emperor Ashoka in north India in the third century BCE, that is about 2,300 years ago, we get the earliest written evidence about some rulers in Tamil Nadu.

Ashoka, who belonged to the Maurya dynasty, was ruling over a very large empire in north India which is known as the Magadhan Empire. This empire covered almost the whole of north India and stretched as far as modern Afghanistan. Ashoka's armies were powerful enough to march southwards and conquer the territory of Tamil Nadu but a sudden change of policy prevented that from happening.

Ashoka's conquests

The reign of Ashoka is of great significance to the history of Tamil Nadu. It was in his reign that the way was opened for the flow of Buddhist and other non-Vedic religious influences into Tamil Nadu. The results of this could be seen in the later centuries. It was in the time of Ashoka's grandfather, Chandragupta Maurya, that the north Indian armies began pushing towards the south. At one point the Mauryan armies reached the northern borders of the Tamil land. When Ashoka became ruler, he was very ambitious and wanted to conquer neighbouring kingdoms to become the emperor of the whole of India. He was victorious in many wars but had to fight hard against the kingdom of Kalinga (in eastern India). Many thousands died before the kingdom was conquered by Ashoka.

Ashoka's Dhamma

The war against Kalinga was his last one. He felt very sad at the death of thousands of people and was, we are told, comforted by a Buddhist monk. His devotion to Buddhism increased and, what is more, he realised the foolishness of waging violent wars. He decided to rule his empire by adopting a policy of non-violence and peace. He called this policy Dhamma. He explained this policy to the people of his empire as well as to those in neighbouring areas through several inscriptions on specially prepared rocks and huge stone pillars.

Ashoka and Tamil rulers

Beyond Ashoka's empire, in the south, was Tamil Nadu. He sent his officials to at least four of the rulers in Tamil Nadu. They were rulers belonging to the Chera, Chola, Pandya and the Atiyaman clans. Officials were also sent to Sri Lanka. This information is recorded in two of Ashoka's inscriptions. This is the earliest information we have regarding political relations between a north Indian king and rulers in Tamil Nadu. Ashoka's actions opened the way for increased flow of influences from the north. Buddhist monks from the north came to south India and Sri Lanka to spread the teachings of the Buddha and establish Buddhist monasteries. More Jain and Ajivika monks also no doubt came to Tamil Nadu during this period. It is said that Ashoka himself built a Buddhist stupa in Kanchipuram. When the Chinese Buddhist monk Xuanzang visited Kanchipuram in the seventh century CE, nearly a thousand years after Ashoka's reign, the Buddhists in that city showed him a stupa which they believed was built by Ashoka.

Jains

The Jain monks who came to Tamil Nadu began the practice of writing inscriptions in their cave shelters giving information about the donors of the shelters and the monks to whom these were donated. These are the earliest stone records that we get in Tamil Nadu.

Tamil Poems

About the same time poets composed a large number of long and short poems which provide valuable information about the people, their culture and their rulers. These are now well known as the Sangam poems. They form a very valuable source for the study of the history of this period.

Tamil Poems

Many poets sang the praises of the rulers and received valuable gifts from them. Two of the famous poets of this period were Kapilar and Paranar. The best of these early Tamil poems were carefully selected and brought together in two collections (anthologies). They are known as *Eddu- thokai* (Eight Collections) and *Paththu- paaddu* (Ten Songs).

Kings, chiefs and poets

At the dawn of history Tamil Nadu was a land filled with various groups of people. One language, Tamil, was dominant in the region. There were many chiefdoms, large and small. Among the major ruling clans were the Pandyas, Cholas, Cheras and the Atiyamans.

Among the rulers who had gained fame as a result of their achievements were the Chera Neduncheral Athan, the Chola Karikalan, the Pandya Muthukudumi Peruvaluthi and the Atiyaman chief Neduman Anchi.

There was constant conflict among the rulers. Many small chiefdoms were conquered by the more powerful chiefs. The result was the emergence of three main kingdoms. These were the kingdoms of the Pandyas, the Cholas and the Cheras. But the whole of Tamil Nadu was not united under one rule.

Foreign Trade

Traders came from the Roman Empire and West Asia to get the spices of Tamil Nadu. They were called Yavanar in Tamil. They came to the ancient ports of Muchiri (west coast), Korkai (south coast) and Puhar (Kaveri-pattinam on the east coast). Pepper was the main spice they wanted.

In return they gave Roman gold coins and wine. Some of the Yavanar served as bodyguards for rulers in Tamil Nadu. They were probably brought as slaves from the Roman Empire. Roman gold coins brought by the Yavanar traders have been found in several places in Tamil Nadu.

Agriculture and Irrigation

The development of rice cultivation and the construction of small reservoirs to irrigate rice fields were notable activities in this period. More than 8,000 years ago, the Yangzi valley in China was one of the first places where the domestication of rice took place. By 3500 BCE rice farming spread to southern China. From there it spread to Southeast Asia. By 2300 BCE rice farming spread to Thailand. About 3000 years ago it spread to south India and Sri Lanka. Soon rice became the staple diet of the people of this region. Rice farming, along with cattle-keeping, brought about a big change in the hunter-gatherer lifestyle of the people. Since plenty of water was needed for rice cultivation, village chiefs paid much attention to the supply of water to the villagers. This led to the construction of small tanks or reservoirs. As the small chiefdoms grew into large kingdoms, one of the main ideals of the rulers was to ensure an adequate supply of water for rice cultivation through the construction of tanks and dams. There are legends about some of the rulers who were successful in fulfilling this duty. The Chola king Karikalan is a hero in some of these legends.

Ashoka's Rock Edict II

The Second Rock Edict issued by Emperor Ashoka provides information about the relations the emperor had with the rulers in Tamil Nadu. This is the earliest inscription in which the major ruling clans of Tamil Nadu (the Cholas, Cheras, Pandyas and the Atiyamans) are mentioned.

Translated Text

Everywhere in the dominions of King Devanampriya Piyadasi (Ashoka), as well as in the border territories of the Chodas (Cholas), Padas (Pandyas), Satyaputa (Atiyaman), Ketalaputa (Cheraman), even Tambapanni (Sri Lanka), the Yona (Greek) king Antiyaka (Antiochos), and also the kings who are the neighbours of this Antiyaka, everywhere provision has been made by King Devanampriya Piyadasi for two kinds of medical treatment, (namely) treatment for humans and treatment for animals. Medicinal herbs suitable for humans and animals were imported and planted wherever they were not previously available. Wells have been dug and trees planted along the roads for the use of humans and animals.

Ashokan Pillar with inscription

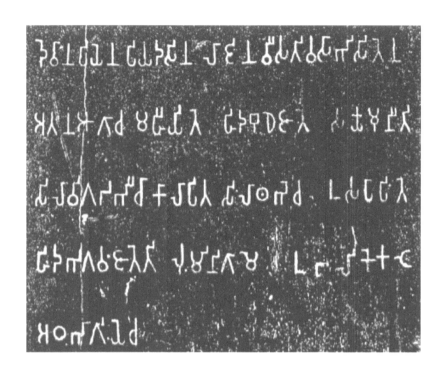

Ashoka's inscription at Lumbini (Nepal), the birthplace of the Buddha

A Sangam Poem

Purananuru 192

யாதும் ஊரே யாவரும் கேளிர்
தீதும் நன்றும் பிறர் தர வாரா
நோதலும் தணிதலும் அவற்றோரன்ன
சாதலும் புதுவது அன்றே, வாழ்தல்
இனிது என மகிழ்ந்தன்றும் இலமே, முனிவின்
இன்னாது என்றலும் இலமே, மின்னொடு
வானம் தண்துளி தலைஇ ஆனாது
கல்பொருது இரங்கும் மல்லற் பேர் யாற்று
நீர் வழிப்படூஉம் புணை போல, ஆருயிர்
முறை வழிப்படூஉம் என்பது திறவோர்
காட்சியில் தெளிந்தனம் ஆகலின், மாட்சியின்
பெரியோரை வியத்தலும் இலமே
சிறியோரை இகழ்தல் அதனினும் இலமே.

Every village is our village, everyone is our relative
Good and bad in life do not happen to us because of others
In the same way, our suffering and the removal of suffering
Cannot be attributed to others
Death is not anything new
We do not rejoice when life is pleasant
We do not say that life is miserable when we are angry
From what those who know have said
We understand that precious life proceeds on its journey
Like a boat sailing down a roaring river
Into which the sky, with lightning strikes, pours down
Cool water, crashing into the rocks.
We, therefore, do not look in amazement at the excellence
of those who are great,
Nor do we look down upon the less fortunate.

Classical Tamil Literature

The collection of Tamil poems, commonly known as Sangam literature, forms the oldest literature in any of the living languages of India. It is also the earliest body of secular poems in India. On account of its antiquity and literary quality, Tamil is now recognized as a classical language. Scholars well-versed in many classical as well as modern languages have rated the Tamil language and its rich literature very highly.

Prof. George L. Hart, a scholar well-versed in Sanskrit and Tamil as well as Latin and Greek and other languages, makes this assessment of the Tamil language and its literature:

"Let me state unequivocally that, by any criteria one may choose, Tamil is one of the great classical literatures and traditions of the world…the quality of classical Tamil literature is such that it is fit to stand beside the great literatures of Sanskrit, Greek, Latin, Chinese, Persian and Arabic."

Ancient Hero Stones. From very ancient times, erecting memorial stones for heroes who died in battle or cattle raids was a common practice. This continued well into the time of the Chola empire.

Tamil-Brahmi Cave Inscriptions
(eye copies)

Inscriptions from Mangulam

Inscriptions from Jambai

Inscriptions from Pugalur

Section 3 *Dawn of History*

2   Retrieval of the Early Historic Past

Some of the Scholars behind the Recovery of Tamil Nadu's Ancient Past

More than 200 years ago when not much was known about the ancient history and literature of Tamil Nadu, a few scholars made valuable contributions to save the written records that were the sources for this history. The English East India Company was ruling the land and the ancient Tamil books were still in the form of palm leaf manuscripts. They were scattered in various homes and many of them were on the verge of being destroyed by white ants. At that time a few of the British officers in the service of the Company took a personal interest in collecting and preserving these manuscripts.

Colin Mackenzie

The earliest and perhaps the best known of these collectors was Colin Mackenzie (1753 – 1821). He collected a vast number of manuscripts, mostly in Telugu but also in Tamil, and saved many of those from destruction. This collection, known as the Mackenzie Collection, is a treasure-house for researchers.

Francis Ellis

From the point of view of Tamil manuscripts, an important contribution was made by the officer Francis Whyte Ellis (1777 – 1815), better known among the Tamil scholars of his time as Ellis *durai.* Ellis made a valuable contribution towards the establishment of the College of Fort St. George (known in Tamil as the Chennai Kalvi Sangam), where he and his Tamil pandit assistants not only collected manuscripts but also edited and published them. Ellis himself edited and published a good part of the *Thirukural* as early as 1812. In the course of their scholarly work, Ellis and his assistants were able to establish that the south Indian languages belonged to a separate family (though they did not call it Dravidian). This was forty years before Bishop Caldwell came up with the identification of the Dravidian family of languages.

C.W. Thamotharam Pillai

Then came the well known local editors. The first of them was C.W. Thamotharam Pillai (1832 – 1901), a scholar from Jaffna (Sri Lanka). He was one of the first two graduates of the University of Madras (the other graduate was also from Jaffna). While working in Tamil Nadu, he developed an early interest in collecting, editing and publishing ancient Tamil texts that were in the form of palm leaf manuscripts. Among the texts he edited were the *Tholkappiyam* and the *Kalithokai.*

C.W. Thamotharam Pillai (1832 – 1901)

U.V. Swaminatha Iyer

U.V. Swaminatha Iyer (1855 – 1942)

He was followed by U.V. Swaminatha Iyer (1855 – 1942) who earned a legendary reputation for the tireless and laborious work he did to save Tamil manuscripts, edit them with great care and publish them. The Tamil epics of *Cheevaka-chinthamani* and *Manimekalai* as well as the classical *Paththupaddu* and *Purananuru* were among the many ancient texts edited and published by him.

James Prinsep, The Scholar Who Deciphered the Brahmi Script

Nearly 250 years ago when the English established their power in Bengal and began to build their empire in the east, the ancient history of India was not known to them. Some of the young British administrators serving in Bengal and other parts of India were curious to find out about India's ancient past. These young men saw hundreds of inscriptions on stone but failed to find anyone who could read them. Ashoka, the greatest emperor of ancient India, was unknown to the Indian pundits. In this situation, several young Europeans learnt

Sanskrit, Pali and other Indian languages, collected valuable manuscripts and made attempts to read the stone inscriptions. These men made an enormous contribution to recover the lost history of South Asia.

James Prinsep (1799-1840)

One of the most renowned of these young men was James Prinsep. He was born in England in August 1799. At the age of twenty, he went to Kolkata to work with the English East India Company. It was a time when many other young British men in India were showing a keen interest in the country's past and discovering ruins of ancient buildings as well as inscriptions. Prinsep quickly developed a deep interest in these matters. He learnt Indian languages, studied some of the newly-discovered ancient Indian coins and wrote about them. From this he went on to decipher the ancient Brahmi script in 1837. This enabled him to read the inscriptions of Ashoka that had been already discovered in various parts of India. Prinsep's achievement helped to read the oldest inscriptions of India and Sri Lanka. Though not immediately, it eventually led to the successful reading of the cave inscriptions in Tamil Nadu.

Prinsep died at a young age, in 1840.

Tamil Inscriptions

It is estimated that there are more than 60,000 inscriptions on stone in temples and other places in Tamil Nadu. These form a valuable treasure for historical research. Many epigraphists (those who study inscriptions) have helped to read and interpret them. Their valuable work began more than 150 years ago. Among the earliest of these scholars who spent time to have the inscriptions copied, read and translated into English was a German Indologist (scholars of Indian languages, history and culture) named Eugen Hultzsch (1857 – 1927). He had the Tamil inscriptions of Rajaraja I in the Thanjavur temple copied, read and translated in the early volumes of the *South Indian Inscriptions.* His work was followed by V. Venkayya and many other Tamil Nadu epigraphists.

Tamil-Brahmi Cave Records come to Life

For more than a hundred years after the Ashokan inscriptions were successfully deciphered and used for historical research, a number of cave records written in Tamil- Brahmi in Tamil Nadu remained unread and unresearched. Iravatham Mahadevan (1930 – 2018), with great dedication and perseverance, devoted his life to the study of these records and very successfully read them all as Old Tamil records, the oldest on stone in Tamil. His contribution to the promotion of interest in ancient Tamil inscriptions is immeasurable.

Legend of the Three Sangams

This is an ancient story about three *sangams* (literary academies) that flourished in Madurai, under the patronage of the Pandya rulers, thousands of years ago. According to this story, the First Sangam was established in the original capital Madurai (later known as Ten Madurai) which was destroyed by a deluge (tsunami). Eighty-nine Pandya kings were associated with the First Sangam. Altogether there were 549 members of this Sangam, beginning with Akattiyanar (Agastya) and including the gods Shivan and Murukan. Under them altogether 4,449 poets composed poems. The First Sangam lasted for 4,400 years.

The Middle Sangam was established in Kapadapuram, the second capital of the Pandyas. Fifty-nine Pandya rulers were associated with this Sangam. There were 59 members, including Tholkaapiyanar. Altogether 3,700 poets composed poems. This Sangam lasted for 3,700 years. Kapadapuram was also destroyed by a deluge.

The Last Sangam was established in the new capital Northern Madurai. Forty- nine Pandya rulers were associated with this Sangam. There were 49 members, including Nakkiranar. Altogether 449 poets composed poems. This Sangam was there for 1,850 years.

Sangam Literature

The earliest Tamil poems collected together in the anthologies called *Eddu- thokai* (Eight Anthologies) and *Paththu- paaddu* (Ten Songs) are considered to form the Sangam literature.

The eight books in the *Eddu-thokai* are:

1. Narrinai (நற்றிணை)
2. Kuruntokai (குறுந்தொகை)
3. Ainkurunuru (ஐங்குறுநூறு)
4. Patirruppattu (பதிற்றுப்பத்து)
5. Paripatal (பரிபாடல்)
6. Kalittokai (கலித்தொகை)
7. Akananuru (அகநானூறு)
8. Purananuru (புறநானூறு)

The ten books in the *Paththu-paaddu* are:

1. Tirumurukarruppatai
   (திருமுருகாற்றுப்படை)

2. Porunararruppatai
   (பொருநராற்றுப்படை)

3. Cirupanarruppatai
   (சிறுபாணாற்றுப்படை)

4. Perumpanarruppatai
   (பெரும்பாணாற்றுப்படை)

5. Mullaippattu (முல்லைப்பாட்டு)

6. Maturaikkanci (மதுரைக்காஞ்சி)

7. Netunalvatai (நெடுநல்வாடை)

8. Kurincippattu (குறிஞ்சிப்பாட்டு)

9. Pattinappalai (பட்டினப்பாலை)

10. Malaipatukatam (மலைபடுகடாம்)

Greco-Roman (Yavana) Trade

Many books written in Greek and Latin in the first and second centuries CE have information about the trade carried on by those who came to Tamil Nadu from the Roman Empire and West Asia. The following is an extract from one of these books, called *Periplus Maris Erythraei:*

'Ships in these ports of trade [in Tamil Nadu] carry full loads because of the volume and quantity of pepper and malabathron. They offer a market for mainly a great amount of money; ... multi-coloured textiles; sulphide of antimony; coral; raw glass; copper; tin; lead; wine ... They also export: good supplies of fine quality pearls; Chinese (silk) cloth; Gangetic nard; malabathron, brought here from the interior; all kinds of transparent gems; diamonds; sapphires; tortoise shell...' (Translation by Lionel Casson)

Some poems in the Sangam collections refer to the Yavanas and their trade in the ports of Tamil Nadu. The following is what is stated in *Akananuru* :

'சேரலர்
சுள்ளியம் பேரியாற்று வெண்நுரை கலங்க
யவனர் தந்த வினைமாண் நன்கலம்
பொன்னொடு வந்து கறியொடு பெயரும்
வளங்கெழு முசிறி'.

'The prosperous Musiri (port) of the Cheralar, where the white foam of the large Sulli River is churned by the well-designed ships of the Yavanas that arrive with gold and depart laden with pepper.'

Karikal Cholan

The Most Famous of the Early Kings

Of the many kings about whom we get information in the Sangam poems and inscriptions, the most famous is undoubtedly the Chola ruler Karikalan. His achievements are mentioned in a number of poems. Many legends about him are found in later inscriptions and books. These are in Tamil, Sanskrit and Telugu. Poets wrote about him even as late as the seventeenth century. He is still remembered in folk legends not only in Tamil Nadu but also in Sri Lanka.

Karikalan was the son of Ilam Chedchenni (Chedchenni the Younger). His name (meaning 'the one with a black or charred leg') is explained in traditions as the result of an injury from a fire accident in his childhood. His father seems to have died when Karikalan was very young, making him heir to the throne at an early age. But his enemies prevented him from becoming king and put him in prison. He escaped from prison,

45

fought his enemies and became ruler.

Karikalan was a great warrior. He fought and defeated many chiefs, including the Aruvalar, Oliyar and eleven Velir chiefs. But his biggest victory was at the Battle of Venni in which he defeated both the Chera and Pandya rulers. He also fought against some chiefs on the northern border of Tamil Nadu. Later traditions credit him with victories over some north Indian rulers as well.

His greatest achievements were in the economic sphere. In the Sangam poems and in all the later legends he is credited with clearing forests for settlement and agriculture and constructing reservoirs and embankments, especially at the Kaveri River. His success in raising the flood-banks of the mighty Kaveri is glorified in many of the later sources. Folk traditions in Sri Lanka refer to the Chola ruler taking away prisoners from the island to construct irrigation works in Tamil Nadu. On account of his contribution towards increasing food production, he is often referred to in the poems as Karikal Peru-valaththaan and Peru-vala Karikal (*peru valam* = great fertility or prosperity).

Karikalan is also remembered as a patron of poets and Brahmanas. He gave lavish gifts to poets. It is said in a late Tamil poem that the king gave 12 lakh gold pieces to the poet who composed the *Paddinappaalai* in his honour. Karikalan is also credited with performing Vedic sacrifices.

Keeladi excavations

Important work relating to the recovery of the Early Historic past of Tamil Nadu is currently being undertaken by archaeologists in Keeladi, near the ancient capital of Madurai. Already, the dating of some of the artefacts excavated here shows that the site may date back to about 500 BCE or earlier. In this respect, the discovery of this site is clearly the most important archaeological discovery in Tamil Nadu in recent years. Brick structures, articles of foreign trade and many other interesting finds indicate that the archaeologists are in the process of uncovering the remains of one of the earliest urban centres in Tamil Nadu.

What Writing did the Ancients Use?

Did you know that all the scripts of the modern Indian languages (except that of Urdu) are derived from a common script? It is called Brahmi and is very simple. (See Fig. below) It is very easy to write and can be learnt quickly. It was a brilliant invention of the ancients. But over the centuries it changed in different regions and today the scripts derived from Brahmi are rather complicated and take time to learn. In Europe, the Roman script (in which English is now written) was kept without major changes for over 2,000 years and today different European languages are written in the same

Roman script. If the people of India (as well as those of Sri Lanka and Southeast Asia where the same Brahmi script became the mother of the Sinhala, Thai, Cambodian, Burmese and Lao scripts) had kept Brahmi without changes, what a difference it would have made today!

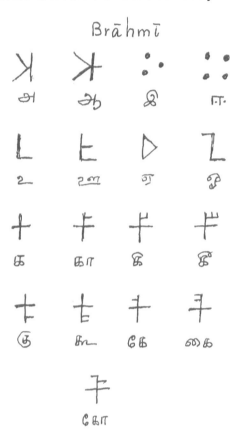

The Brahmi script in the third century BCE

Date	Sinhala	Tamil
200 BCE	╬	╬
100 BCE	╬	╬
200 CE	ℐ	╬
500 CE	℉	℉
1000 CE	中	℉
1500 CE	ක	ก

How the Brahmi letter ✛ (ka) changed in Sinhala and Tamil

Syrian Christians

Christians have been living in Tamil Nadu from ancient times. A community of Christians, known as the Syrian Christians, who live in Kerala, trace their origin to a group converted to Christianity, according to their traditions, in the first century CE by St. Thomas (a disciple of Jesus Christ). There were Syrian Christians in Sri Lanka, too, in the early centuries CE, with a priest ordained in Persia (Iran). The Nestorian Christians were based in Persia. In Kerala, too, the Church in Persia provided the priests in the fourth century CE and later. There were also, no doubt, Christian traders from the west settled in the ports of Kerala.

A Nestorian Cross

Jews in Ancient Tamil Nadu

Members of the Jewish community were also among the early West Asian settlers in the west coast of ancient Tamil Nadu. It is claimed that some of them came as traders in the time of King Solomon nearly 3,000 years ago. There is a strong tradition that Jewish settlers came to the west coast after the destruction of their famous temple in Jerusalem in 70 CE. Jewish traders continued to live in the ports of Kerala for several centuries. A copper plate charter issued by the Kerala ruler Kulasekhara about the year 1000 CE to a Jewish merchant named Joseph Rabban in Kerala provides unmistakable evidence of Jewish settlements.

What did the Ancients Use as Writing Material?

For nearly 2,500 years, palm leaves were used as writing material. How did they write on palm leaves? This is how they prepared the leaves. Young leaves of the palmyrah palm (sometimes the leaves of the talipot palm) are the most suitable for writing on, since the more mature leaves are brittle when dry. These leaves are cut to the required size (usually about 6 cm wide and about 50 cm long, although talipot leaf manuscripts can be wider and longer). Traditionally these leaves were first boiled in water to make them soft and then dried in the shade. When dry, the pieces are pressed, polished and trimmed. A hole is made in the centre through which a cord is passed, when the writing is completed, and all the leaves of a book are tied together. Two thin wooden planks or panels, slightly larger in size than the leaves, are used as covers.

Writing on the leaf was done with a metal stylus (a sharply pointed tool for writing or marking). Fresh green leaves were rubbed on the manuscript to make the writing more visible. Writing on leaves required special skills and plenty of practice. It was a specialised job, the work of scribes. Some families specialised in this and passed on the skills from generation to generation. It is said that palm leaf manuscripts could last for about three centuries. But there were always many threats. Often white ants destroyed the manuscripts. Natural herbs, margosa leaves or certain types of oil (like citronella) were used to keep insects away. When the manuscripts decayed, they were copied on fresh leaves. This was how ancient Tamil books (some 2,000 years old) were preserved until they were printed in modern times. The copyists and scribes who worked hard to preserve these ancient and valuable treasures are the unsung heroes of Tamil Nadu's literary history.

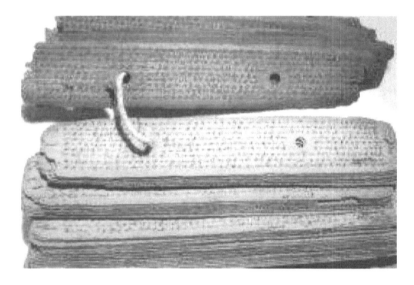

A Palm leaf manuscript

Section 4 *Dominance of Buddhism and Jainism*

1 The Pallavas

In the third century BCE Emperor Ashoka refers to the Cholas, Pandyas, Cheras and the Atiyamans as prominent rulers in Tamil Nadu. For the next six centuries Tamil poems tell us about the bitter conflicts among these rulers. None of them succeeded in uniting the whole of Tamil Nadu and creating a powerful kingdom. The Chola ruler Karikalan appears to have come close to being the overlord of Tamil Nadu after defeating his main rivals, the Pandya and Chera kings, as well as many less powerful chiefs. But he did not unite the whole of Tamil Nadu.

The Kalabhras

By the end of the third century CE the rise of a powerful kingdom in neighbouring Andhra led to new political pressures from the north. This was the kingdom of the Satavahanas. The expansion of their power towards the south seems to have pushed some clans to seek their fortunes in Tamil Nadu. Very little is known about the political conditions in Tamil Nadu between 300 CE and 500 CE. Nothing is known about the Cholas, Pandyas and the Cheras. They appear to have lost their authority. A new clan from outside appears to have seized power in some parts of Tamil Nadu.

This new clan is known as the Kalabhras. They have not left any record of their rule. As a result, not much is known about their activities except that some of the Kalabhra rulers were patrons of Buddhism or were opposed to Brahmins.

The Pallavas

When the Kalabhras were in Tamil Nadu another clan was

also moving from Andhra into the area north of Kanchipuram. They are known to us as the Pallavas. By the middle of the fourth century CE they established their power in Kanchi and began to extend their power further south. About the same time, in the south, members of the old Pandya clan defeated the Kalabhra rulers and began a new period of Pandya rule. Over the next couple of centuries, the Pallavas and the Pandyas fought each other for dominance in Tamil Nadu.

In the time of Pallava rule remarkable developments took place in various areas. These contributed to the evolution of Tamil Nadu's separate culture. The foundation for the unique temple architecture of the south was laid in this period. Four major religions – Jainism, Buddhism, Saivism and Vaishnavism – flourished during this period. Remarkable developments took place in Tamil language and literature. Sanskrit learning, too, gained importance. Trade and cultural contacts with Southeast Asia were promoted by mercantile communities based in Tamil Nadu. Monks from Tamil Nadu helped to spread Buddhism in China. Of great significance was the development of irrigation technology which later led to the construction of some of the largest human-made reservoirs in the ancient world.

Mahendravarman I 580 – 630 CE

A Versatile Pallava Ruler

Mahendravarman I who ruled from Kanchi at the beginning of the seventh century CE was one of the greatest Pallava kings. He could be described as one of the most colourful and accomplished personalities in the early history of Tamil Nadu. He was a powerful king, a warrior, tank-builder, Sanskrit scholar, poet, playwright, painter, musician, religious revivalist and innovator in the field of architecture – that is the profile of the king that we get from the sources we have.

Mahendravarman ruled a large part of northern Tamil Nadu. It is not possible to determine the exact extent of kingdoms in ancient times. It appears that he ruled an area that included some parts of southern Andhra and extended up to the Kaveri River. The rising power of the Chalukyas in Andhra did not leave him in peace. The Chalukya ruler claims to have defeated Mahendravarman. But the Pallava records say that Mahendravarman defeated the Chalukya in a battle near Kanchi. It is possible that the two fought several battles, some of which were won by Mahendravarman.

Mahendravarman is more renowned for his achievements in the arts of peace. It was in his time that the first stone temples, excavated out of rocks, were constructed in Tamil Nadu. These are mainly cave temples. Most of them are Shiva temples. A few are dedicated to Vishnu. The best examples of these cave temples are found in Mandagappattu, Pallavaram, Mamandur and Thiruchchirappalli.

He was well-versed in Sanskrit and wrote plays in that language. *Mattavilasa-prahasana* is one of the plays written by him. The irrigation tank called Mahendra-tadakam was probably built by him. He had several titles which reveal the different areas of interest he had. One of the titles is *Chittirakkara-puli (a tiger among painters)* which shows his talent as a painter. He was also involved with the Shaiva revival activities, known as the Bhakthi movement, that was going on in his time. He was a Jain when he became king but was converted to Shaivism by the famous Shaiva saint Appar.

Mandagapattu : The earliest rock - cut cave temple in Tamil Nadu

Mamandur : Rock - cut cave temple

Bodhidharma

The monk who sailed from Kanchi to China to become the Founder of Zen Buddhism

In the early centuries of Pallava rule, Kanchi was a renowned centre of Buddhism. Monks from China, Sri Lanka and Central Asia came to this city while monks from Kanchi sailed to Southeast Asia and China to spread the message of the Buddha. Undoubtedly the most famous of the Buddhist monks who went forth to the eastern lands from Tamil Nadu was Bodhidharma (known in China as Tamo and in Japan as Daruma). He is popularly considered to be the founder of Zen Buddhism (known in Sanskrit as *Dhyāna Mārga* and in Chinese as *Ch'an*).

What we know of Bodhidharma is from Chinese records. According to some of the more popular Chinese traditions, he lived in the sixth century and was the son of a king of Kanchi. As in the case of many important personalities, several legends have grown around Bodhidharma and this makes it difficult to know the real details of his life. It may be of interest to add that Chinese traditions credit Bodhidharma with the founding of the martial arts at the Shaolin Temple in China.

Daruma (Ta-mo, Bodhidharma) - A Japanese Drawing

Xuanzang

The Chinese Monk who visited Kanchi in 634 CE

As Buddhism spread widely in China, several Chinese monks undertook the very difficult journey to India to visit the Buddhist sites, learn at the leading Buddhist monasteries and to collect Buddhist texts for translation into Chinese. A few of them wrote about their experiences when they returned to China and have remained famous to this day because of the value of their writings as sources of history. One of the earliest of these scholarly monks was Faxian (spelt earlier as Fa Hien).

Xuanzang (a later painting)

He began his long journey in 399 CE, travelled overland through Central Asia, spent several years in India and then sailed to Sri Lanka. After staying at Anuradhapura for two years, he returned to China by ship in 412 CE at the age of

77. Another Chinese Buddhist monk named Xuanzang came to India in the seventh century in search of Buddhist texts. He too wrote about his travels and experiences. He travelled widely in India and visited Kanchi in 634 CE. The visit took place in the reign of Pallava Narasim- havarman I. The following is what he had recorded about the kingdom which he called Ta-lo-pi-ch'a (Dravida):

"This country is about 6000 li (one li = about 500 metres) in circuit; the capital of the country is called Kanchipura (Kin-chi-pu-lo), and is about 30 li round. The soil is fertile and regularly cultivated, and produces abundance of grain. There are also many flowers and fruits. It produces precious gems and other articles. The climate is hot, the character of the people courageous. They are deeply attached to the principles of honesty and truth, and highly esteem learning; in respect of their language and written characters, they differ but little from those of Mid-India. There are some hundred of *sangharamas* and 10,000 priests. They all study the teaching of the Sthavira (Chang-tso-pu) school belonging to the Great Vehicle. There are some eighty Deva temples, and many heretics called Nigranthas. Tathagata [the Buddha] in olden days, when living in the world, frequented this country much; he preached the law [dharma] here and converted men, and therefore Asoka-raja built stupas over all the sacred spots where these traces exist. The city of Kanchipura is the native place of Dharmapala Bodhisattva … To the south of the city not a great way is a large *sangharama,* in which men of the same sort, renowned for talent and learning assemble and stop. There is a stupa about 100 feet high which was built by Asoka-raja.

(Translation: Samuel Beal)

Section 4 *Dominance of Buddhism and Jainism*

2   Buddhist and Jain Scholars

After the time of Ashoka, Buddhism and Jainism were firmly established in Andhra and Karnataka. But it took a long time for them to become popular in Tamil Nadu. Major rulers of Tamil Nadu do not seem to have embraced these religions and this may have been one of the reasons for this situation. With the coming of the Kalabhras, who are known to have supported Buddhism, this situation began to change. There were Buddhists and Jains among the Pallava rulers. Some Pandya rulers may also be said to have patronized Jainism.

Buddhism

Whether the rulers in Tamil Nadu showed their support to these religions by building monasteries or other monuments, as those in Karnataka and Andhra did, is hard to say. But there were Buddhist and Jain monasteries in the capital cities and major ports. Buddhist stupas were also built in many places. By the time Xuanzang, the Chinese Buddhist monk, visited Kanchi early in the seventh century, there were many Buddhist monasteries and stupas in that city. He also says that there was a stupa built by Ashoka. According to this Chinese monk, there were thousands of Buddhist monks and many Jains in Kanchi. It is known that in the Chola capital of Uraiyur and the port of Kaveripattinam as well as Nagapattinam there were Buddhist monasteries.

Buddhist scholars

In these monasteries resided many Tamil, Pali and Sanskrit scholars. The Pali scholars were followers of the Theravada school of Buddhism while the Sanskrit scholars were Mahayana Buddhists. Two of the famous monks from Tamil

Nadu who wrote books in Pali were Buddhadatta and Dhammapala. Another famous Pali scholar, Buddhaghosa (not from Tamil Nadu) wrote Pali books while residing in the monasteries of Kanchi and Mayura- rupa-pattana (identified as Mylapore). Many of the Mahayana scholars were residents of monasteries in Kanchi. The most famous of them was Dignaga. It is said that he was a native of Siyamangalam (a village south of Kanchi). He studied at the renowned Buddhist centre popularly known as the Nalanda University in north India and returned to live in a monastery in Kanchi. He was well known as a debater and philosopher. He wrote some important books on philosophy in Sanskrit.

There are no remains of the great Theravada monasteries and Mahayana temples of ancient Tamil Nadu. The only example of a Tamil Buddhist palli preserved even in ruins is the Rajaraja-perumpalli (Velgam Vehera) near Trincomalee in Sri Lanka. The impressive remains of this monastery, with a number of Chola inscriptions, cover an extensive area. 11th century.

No Mahayana Temple has survived in Tamil Nadu. There is in Sri Lanka a Mahayana Temple in the late Pallava style, built entirely of stone. It is known as the Nalanda Gedige

Buddhist epics

Some of the Tamil Buddhist scholars were great Tamil poets. Of the well known five Tamil epics two were written by Buddhist poets. These are the *Manimekalai* (written by Sattanar) and the *Kundalakeci* (written by Nathakuttanar). Only *Manimekalai* has survived in full.

Jainism

Jaina monasteries were very widespread in Tamil Nadu and schools in these monasteries contributed to the development of education. The Tamil word *palli* for school has come down to us from the time monasteries *(palli)* were functioning as schools. Jain poets contributed to Tamil literature from very early times. Two of the most popular ancient Tamil books written by poets associated with Jainism are the *Naladiyar* and the *Thirukural.* The Jains also produced three of the five Tamil epics: *Silappathikaram, Cheevakachintamani* and *Valaiyapathi.* The last one is completely lost.

The Thirukural - A Great Work on Ethics

One of the most widely admired of the ancient Tamil texts is the *Thirukural.* It is also perhaps the one that has had the greatest influence on the people of Tamil Nadu. It has been translated into many non-Indian languages since 1730 (when it was translated into Latin). The following is one of the many comments made by world leaders on this famous work of Thiruvalluvar:

"There hardly exists in the literature of the world a collection of maxims in which we find so much of lofty wisdom…

Valluvar believed that in this very natural world, the liberated man can find his heaven and said that perfect bliss could be attained by an individual in this world itself and it is unnecessary to wait indefinitely for the transformation of the world in order to transform oneself. Thus, he took life and world affirmation to a loftier plane than Christ did…

With sure stroke, the Kural draws the ideal of simple ethical humanity."

Albert Schweitzer (1875-1965), 20th century Christian philosopher, missionary, humanitarian, Nobel Peace Prize winner and a great exponent of the concept of Reverence for Life.

Maxims for Students: Thirukural

No: 391
Learn, what is to be learnt, without flaws;
Once learnt stand by what you learned.

No: 396
The more you dig the more water will flow from a well in the sand;
The more you learn, the more knowledge will flow.

Jaina Monuments

Jaina Cave Temple : Chitharal. Unlike the Buddhist monuments, many ancient monuments of the Jainas have survived in Tamil Nadu.

Relief sculpture in the Jaina temple at Chitharal

Section 4 *Dominance of Buddhism and Jainism*

3   Clash of Religions – The Bhakthi Movement

The fifth and sixth centuries appear to have seen the peak of Buddhist and Jain influence in Tamil Nadu. Towards the end of the sixth century, the rise of Shaivism and Vaishnavism posed a serious challenge to Buddhism and Jainism. At that time there were two powerful kingdoms in Tamil Nadu, the Pallava kingdom with its capital at Kanchi and the Pandya kingdom which had Madurai as its capital. Both were ruled by Jaina kings. Earlier, the Pallava kingdom had Buddhist kings, too. But about this time Brahmanical influence and activities began to increase. The worship of Shiva and Vishnu soon gained prominence.

The political scene also changed about this time. The Pallavas already held power in northern Tamil Nadu. Their power extended up to the Kaveri river. In the far south the ancient Pandya clan succeeded in defeating the Kalabhras and other enemies and emerged as serious rivals to the Pallavas. For the next two centuries they fought many wars in which the Cholas and the Sinhala rulers in the south as well as the Gangas in Karnataka and others in the north were allies of one or the other rival powers in Tamil Nadu.

Shaiva-Vaishnava revival

While this political conflict went on for nearly three centuries without either the Pandyas or the Pallavas gaining domination over the whole of Tamil Nadu, an important religious activity that brought about major social and cultural developments was taking place all over Tamil Nadu. This is popularly known as the Bhakthi movement. This was a movement of the worshippers of Shiva (Shaivaites) and the worshippers of

Vishnu (Vaishnavaites) aimed at ousting Buddhism and Jainism and promoting the worship of Shiva and Vishnu. It was very emotional and at times violent. After more than three centuries, it resulted in fully achieving its goals – the complete disappearance of Buddhism and the near- extinction of Jainism in Tamil Nadu.

Nayanars

The leaders of the Shaiva movement were known as Nayanars. In the religion of Tamil Nadu before the arrival of the Vedic religion and the religions of the Jains and Buddhists from north India, there was the worship of various local gods. After the spread of the Vedic religion by the Brahmins, the local religious worship (which sometimes included offerings of blood and toddy) was carried on without any attempt to suppress them, while Vedic sacrifices were performed by the Brahmins with royal patronage. The people of Tamil Nadu had their own gods and religious practices before the spread of the religions of north India. Among the major deities were Seyon, Mayon, Korravai and Kadalon.

The higher philosophy of Shaivism, with its rituals performed by Brahmins using the Sanskrit language, was far removed from the folk religion of the ordinary people who used Tamil for their rituals. The ability to accommodate these two types of worship in the same religion ensured the success of the new Shaivism that was evolving at this time.

Conversion of rulers

The Nayanars started their campaign at the very top with the conversion of the two mighty rulers in Tamil Nadu. This has been a successful strategy of religious leaders in other places as well. In nearby Sri Lanka the acceptance of Buddhism by the Anuradhapura ruler Devanampiya Tissa led to the spread of Buddhism over the whole island. The Nayanar named Thirunavukkarasar, popularly known as Appar (Father), succeeded in converting the mighty Pallava Mahendravarman from Jainism to Shaivism. This marked the beginning of the triumphant march of Shaivism throughout the Tamil country. In the Pandya kingdom, another Nayanar named Sambandar, a junior contemporary of Appar, first won over the queen, Mankayarkarasi, and easily brought the Pandya king into the Shaiva fold.

The Nayanars travelled to various sacred sites all over Tamil Nadu with their devoted followers, singing hymns in Tamil and debating with Jains and Buddhists. The monks who lost the debates were punished. The movement went on for over three centuries. At the end of it, 63 Nayanars were recognized as the most prominent leaders of the movement. The most famous were Thirunavukkarasar, Sambandar and Sundaramurthi. There was also a lady by the name of Karaikkal Ammaiyar and a Chera ruler, Cheraman Perumal. Their hymns, known as Devaram, are still sung in temples, schools and at religious gatherings.Another saint, Manikkavacakar, is famous for his *Thiruvasagam* which is highly revered and sung in temples.

Alvars

There were twelve leaders of the Vaishnava movement known as Alvars. Their movement seems to have started very early, possibly in the fifth or sixth century. Among the better known of these Alvars were Thirumangai Alvar, Nammalvar and Thirumalisai Alvar. The only lady in this group was Andal. A Chera ruler, Kulasekhara, was also a prominent Alvar.

Shankara and Ramanuja

In the midst of the Bhakthi movement, the south gave to the whole of India two of the greatest philosophers and thinkers of Hinduism. They were Shankara (8th century) and Ramanuja (11th century). Their teachings, together with Bhakthi devotionalism, spread to the north where these made a deep influence on religious thought and practice.

Decline of Buddhism and Jainism

By the end of the eighth century Jainism and Buddhism were completely subdued. These two religions preached a high moral philosophy and emphasized non-violence. They did not encourage the worship of gods which also meant that there were no elaborate rituals. They did not, therefore, enjoy much support among the ordinary people when the Nayanars and Alvars offered an alternative – devotional worship of gods.

Section 4 *Dominance of Buddhism and Jainism*

4   Kanchipuram – A Centre of Learning

From very early times, nearly 2,000 years ago, Kanchi is known to have been a centre of learning for members of various religions. As early as the fourth century there appears to have been a renowned Sanskrit college *(ghatika)* at this place which was attracting students from distant kingdoms. While this college looked after Vedic studies, the other non-Vedic religions had also established their own monasteries in Kanchi which became centres of learning. In the Tamil epic *Manimekalai,* the heroine is told to go to Kanchi to study the different philosophical systems of the Veda, Shiva, Vishnu, Ajivika, Jaina, Sankhya, Vaiseshika and Lokayata. Kanchi also had Buddhist monasteries, of both the Theravada and Mahayana schools, which flourished for several centuries.

Buddhist scholars

Many renowned scholars studied in Kanchi or worked in centres of learning in Kanchi. Theravada Buddhists considered Kanchi to be one of the three great centres of Theravada learning in south India. One of their greatest Pali commentators, Buddhaghosa, stayed in a Kanchi monastery when he wrote some of his commentaries.

Among the Mahayana Buddhist scholars associated with Kanchi the most famous was Dignaga, the Mahayana philosopher and debater. The Chinese monk Xuanzang, visiting Kanchi early in the seventh century, says that there was a large number of Buddhist monasteries in which 10,000 monks were resident, engaged in studying Buddhism.

Sanskrit scholars

Kanchi was always an important centre for Sanskrit learning. In the time of the Pallavas two renowned Sanskrit poets, Bharavi and Dandin, were in Kanchi. Later, in the time of the Cholas, the famous Vaishnava philosopher Ramanuja, studied in Kanchi.

Mamallapuram – A World Heritage Site
with the largest open-air rock relief in the world

Mamallapuram is an open air art gallery by the sea created by the skilful sculptor- architects of the Pallava kingdom in the seventh and eighth centuries CE. The monolithic and cave temples show the early stages in the evolution of Tamil Nadu's unique temple architecture.The Shore Temple is one of the best examples of the early Pallava temples. Mamallapuram was declared a UNESCO World Heritage Site in 1984.

*Shaiva saint Sundaramurthi Nayanar – bronze image
11th century CE – from a Shiva Temple in Polonnaruva, Sri
Lanka*

Karaikkal Ammaiyar – female Shaiva saint – bronze image, 11th century CE – from a Shiva temple in Polonnaruva, Sri Lanka.

Karaikkal Ammaiyar (whose earlier name was Punithavathi) came from a rich trading family in Karaikkal. She became an ardent devotee of Shiva and decided to spend her life to the service of her Lord. It is said that she prayed to Shiva to remove her female beauty and to grant her the privilege to forever watch him dance. A miracle occurred and she was transformed into an emaciated woman. This figure shows her as an emaciated woman watching Shiva's dance and singing.

Early Pallava Style - Shore Temple , Mamallapuram - 7th century

*Arjuna's Penance / Descent of the Ganga, Mamallapuram
The world's largest open-air rock relief*

*Four famous Buddhist scholars associated with Kanchi
– an artist's impression.
Left to right: Buddhaghosa (Theravada scholar,) Dignaga
(Mahayana scholar, Padmasambhava (Vajrayana scholar,)
Bodhidharma (Dhyana Marga / Zen scholar)*

Other ancient Buddha images in Kanchi

Many Buddha statues that originally belonged to monasteries in ancient Kanchi have been discovered. This statue was in the Kanchi Kamakshi Temple and is now in the Chennai Museum. It is similar in style to the statues in Amaravati (Andhra) and belongs to about the 5th century CE.

Nagapattinam Buddhist Vihara

The last remaining tower of the Nagapattinam Buddhist monastery,
as seen and drawn early in the 19th century.
It was demolished in 1867 to make way for a new building

A king from Indonesia built a Buddhist monastery at Nagapattinam. It was named Chulamanivarma- vihara, after him. Rajaraja Chola I made endowments to this monastery, the details of which were written on copper plates. These plates are in Leiden (Holland) A second grant was made later by Kulottunga Chola and the copper plates giving the details are also in Leiden. By the time of this grant, the vihara also had the name Rajaraja-perumpalli. The seal and plates of the first grant are shown above

Sri Mara Sri Vallabha

A Powerful Pandya Ruler

Among the new Pandya rulers who succeeded in building a powerful kingdom and restoring the honour of their ancient clan after the sixth century, the name of Sri Mara Sri Vallabha shines bright. From the seventh century, the Pallavas and the Pandyas fought for domination in Tamil Nadu and the struggle continued well into the ninth century. Though unable to completely defeat the Pallavas, by the beginning of the ninth century the Pandyas had succeeded in building a powerful kingdom under Varagunavarman, also known as Nedunjadaiyan. His son, Sri Mara Sri Vallabha succeeded him in 815 CE.

As a rising power the Pandyas faced the opposition of not only the Pallavas but also many other minor rulers. The Gangas, Cholas, Kalingas and others allied with the Pallavas and fought Sri Mara at Kudamukku (Kumbakonam). Sri Mara defeated this alliance and took on the title of *Paracakra-kolahala* (Confounder of the Circle of his Enemies).

Sri Lanka was drawn into the conflict between the Pallavas and the Pandyas. Possibly fearing the rising power of the Pandyas, the Sinhalese ruler at Anuradhapura, Sena I, allied with the Pallavas. Sri Mara invaded Sri Lanka and made a successful march to Anuradhapura. Sena fled to the south, leaving the capital open to the attack of the Pandya army. Having taken the royal treasures, the Pandya king sent messengers to Sena, imposed a treaty and left the island.

Events took a different turn in the reign of Sena I's successor Sena II. Sri Mara's son, Varaguna by name, became estranged with his father and sought refuge in the Sinhalese court. This seems to have provided an opportunity for the Pallava ruler and his Sinhalese ally to keep the aggressive Pandya under check. While the Pallava Nrpatungavarman attacked the Pandya territories from the north, provoking Sri Mara to march against him, the Sinhalese ruler sent his army to Madurai from the south. The Pallavas defeated the Pandya army at the Battle of Arisil. In the Pandya capital the Sinhalese army succeeded in overrunning the defences and defeating the depleted Pandya army that rushed back from the Battle of Arisil to save their capital city. What turned out to be more disastrous to the Pandyas was the death of Sri Mara himself. The Sinhalese army placed the Pandya prince Varaguna on the throne at Madurai. This took place in 862 CE.

Section 5 *Tamil Nadu Under One Rule*

1   The Rise of the Cholas

The Chola clan disappeared from the political scene after the third century CE and it took nearly six centuries before someone claiming descent from this ancient clan re-established the rule of the Cholas in the region of Thanjavur. This ruler was Vijayalaya. He began his reign in the middle of the ninth century and the Pallava king was his overlord. By that time Pallava power had declined and Vijayalaya's son Aditya defeated the Pallavas and conquered the latter's territory of Thondaimandalam. This was at the end of the ninth century. With this victory began the spectacular rise of the Cholas.

Parantaka Chola

Aditya's son Parantaka I came to the throne in 905 CE. Under him Chola power expanded in different directions. One of his first victories was against the Pandya ruler who had the ruler of Anuradhapura (Sri Lanka) as his ally. The combined armies of the Pandya and Sri Lanka rulers were defeated by Parantaka. The Pandya ruler fled to Sri Lanka and the kingdom of the Pandyas came under Parantaka's rule. The Chola king was on friendly terms with the Chera ruler, for Parantaka's mother was from the Chera family.

Although he emerged as the most powerful ruler in Tamil Nadu very early in his reign, he had to face the opposition of powerful enemies from the north. The Rashtrakutas were the main enemies of Parantaka. For some time he was able to defend his empire from the attacks of his northern neighbours, but towards the end of his long reign it became increasingly difficult to hold on to the northern parts of the empire. In 949 CE the Rashtrakuta king Krishna III and his allies invaded the

Chola territories and defeated Parantaka at the Battle of Takkolam. A large part of the northern half of the Chola empire was lost.

Rajarajesvara (now Brihadeesvara) Temple built by Rajaraja I, Thanjavur, 11th century.

Rajaraja

Parantaka I died in 955 CE. For nearly three decades after his death, the Cholas struggled with weak successors until Rajaraja I ascended the throne in 985 CE. Considered as the greatest of the Chola rulers, Rajaraja conducted campaigns in almost every direction and again expanded the area under Chola rule. Very early in his reign, he broke the alliance of the three southern kingdoms, namely the kingdoms of the Cheras, Pandyas and the Sinhalas. Then he turned his attention northwards and successfully fought and annexed some kingdoms in Karnataka. With the able assistance of his son Rajendra, the Chola ruler extended his power up to the Tungabhadra River and subdued the rulers in Andhra. For the first time, the whole of Tamil Nadu was under the sway of a single monarch. There was no concept of ethnic nations or national boundaries at that time. It was not, therefore, seen as an achievement of special significance. The conquest and annexation of the Pandya kingdom was as significant as the conquest of Ilam (Sri Lanka). To mark these victories, the Chola rulers were proud to take the title of *'Maturaiyum Ilamum konda'* (Conqueror of Madurai and Ilam).

Temple at Gangaikonda - Cholapuram, built by Rajendra I, 11th century.

Rajaraja Cholan I

Founder of the Chola Empire
and the greatest of the rulers of Tamil Nadu

The Chola prince Arumolivarman, who began his reign in 985 as Rajaraja, was the son of Parantakan Sundara Cholan and Vanavan-mahadevi. With his accession to the throne there began a period of glory and greatness in the history of Tamil Nadu. This lasted for more than a century. In the reign of this ruler we see the work of many powerful forces that resulted in remarkable achievements in various fields.

Internal troubles within the Chola family and the rule of inefficient kings led to the failure of the Cholas to bring the whole of Tamil Nadu under one rule. When Rajaraja became king some of the lost territories in the north (in

Thondaimandalam) had been recovered, but in the south the Pandya and Kerala rulers had allied with the Sinhala ruler in Sri Lanka to give opposition to the Cholas. Rajaraja comprehensively defeated all of them and brought Tamil Nadu under one rule. He then extended his power beyond the borders of Tamil Nadu, including northern Sri Lanka and the Maldives and laid the firm foundations for a powerful empire. This achievement enabled his illustrious son and successor, Rajendra I, to extend the power of the Cholas further with his march towards the Ganga River along the east coast and the naval expeditions to Southeast Asia. Under Rajendra the empire attained its greatest extent.

Rajaraja's conquests brought considerable wealth into Tamil Nadu from the subdued kingdoms. Together with this, the flourishing overseas trade brought prosperity. This greatly helped Rajaraja to promote the development of the arts and to build many temples, including the Rajarajeshvara Temple at Thanjavur. This architectural masterpiece has stood for more than a thousand years showing to the world the heights reached in the field of architecture under Rajaraja. To this great temple Rajaraja assigned as many as four hundred dancing girls and many dance masters and musicians. It is left to our imagination to think of the developments that took place in dance and music in this and other temples at that time.

As an ardent devotee of Shiva, Rajaraja made very rich endowments to the Rajarajeshvara Temple and promoted his religion in many other ways. It was in his time that the hymns of the Shaiva Nayanars were collected and included in the Shaiva canon. He also patronised Buddhism and made a significant endowment to a Buddhist monastery at Nagapattinam at the request of a Southeast Asian ruler. This monastery was later called Rajaraja- perumpalli. Another Buddhist monastery, in Sri Lanka, was also named after Rajaraja. After centuries of conflict between the Shaivaites and the Buddhists, there was religious harmony under Rajaraja.

There is no chronicle giving us the details of Rajaraja's

achievements but his vast stone inscriptions tell us much, prompting the great historian Nilakanta Sastri to pronounce that this monarch was 'the greatest of all the great Cola rulers'.

Overseas conquests

The invasion of Sri Lanka was not the only overseas campaign launched by Rajaraja. After taking control of the Lakshadveep (Laccadive) Islands, his navy attacked the Maldive Islands. This, it seems, was aimed at controlling the Indian Ocean trade. His interest in this trade is seen from the mission he sent to the court of the Chinese emperor. In the north he fought with the Chalukyas and successfully defended his northern borders. Rajaraja died in 1014 CE.

Rajaraja's conquests brought much wealth to the Chola kingdom. This prosperity helped cultural and economic development. Rajaraja built in his capital, Thanjavur, the largest and tallest of all Indian temples, the Rajarajesvaram (popularly known as the Great Temple). Not only architecture, many other arts like sculpture, painting, dancing, music and literature flourished in this period of prosperity inaugurated by Rajaraja. What is less known is the significant developments that took place in hydraulic engineering leading to the construction of large irrigation tanks. These developments culminated in the building of the largest irrigation reservoir in the world, the Veeranam Eri near Jayamkonda- cholapuram.

Chola Painting - Rajarajesvara Temple, Thanjavur, 11th century.
Identified as Rajaraja and his guru.

Nataraja Sculpture Gangaikonda - Cholapuram. 11th century.

Section 5 *Tamil Nadu Under One Rule*

2   Height of Chola Power

The height of Chola power was attained in the reign of Rajaraja's son and successor Rajendra I (1012 – 1044). As a ruler with the power to conduct major expeditions on land and sea, Rajendra made his influence felt beyond the borders of Tamil Nadu – in the kingdoms up to the Ganges in eastern India and in the ports around the Bay of Bengal. Following the footsteps of his father, he appears to have been concerned about the overseas trade that brought considerable wealth to the Chola state. Possibly to remove obstacles to this trade, especially with China, Rajendra sent a naval expedition to some of the major ports of Southeast Asia. No other Indian king had ever undertaken such a task.

March to the North

In the north Rajendra's armies succeeded in annexing some of the southern regions of the Chalukya territories. The most notable military expedition conducted by Rajendra was the march to the Ganges along the eastern seaboard. Bringing water from the Ganges as a symbol of his conquest of the north, he built a new city and named it Gangai-konda-cholapuram (the City of the Chola who conquered the Ganges).

Sri Lanka

In the south, the territories of the Cheras and the Pandyas were under Chola rule. But in Sri Lanka only the northern part had been annexed in Rajaraja's time. Keen on completing the conquest of the island and recovering the Pandya crown jewels left there by Rajasimha (the Pandya king) when he fled to Anuradhapura in the time of Parantaka I, Rajendra sent an expedition to Sri Lanka in 1017 CE. The victorious Chola army took the Sinhalese king prisoner and recovered the Pandya crown jewels.

Imperial Administration

Rajendra introduced a new system of administration to hold together the expanding Chola empire. Already the empire had been divided into *mandalams* or provinces (thus, each conquered kingdom became a *mandalam*). According to the new scheme, the emperor hand- picked the viceroys to govern the provinces, ceremoniously crowned them, conferred on them the respective titles that marked their official appointment and dispatched them to their respective provinces. They were given even new dynastic names that reflected their new status. These names were the result of a novel idea of combining the dynastic name of the former local ruler and that of the emperor (namely, Chola). Thus, the viceroy of the Pandya province assumed the dynastic name of Chola-Pandya. The one who was sent to Kerala was given the name of Chola-Kerala. The viceroy of Sri Lanka took the name of Chola- Lankesvara.

Even with such administrative arrangements the territories under Chola rule could not be held together for long. Towards the end of the reign of Rajendra I the empire faced serious challenges. Rajendra died in 1044 CE and was succeeded by Rajadhiraja I.

Dancing apsaras (female spirit of the clouds), Chola painting, Thanjavur 11th century.
The powerful and flowing lines show the mastery of the painter. The painting also reveals the developments that had taken place in the art of dance in the 11th century.

Section 5 *Tamil Nadu Under One Rule*

3 Society: Education – Temple Schools

Education was always held in high esteem in Tamil Nadu from very early times. The Jaina monks were among the earliest to encourage learning among the ordinary people. Their early hermitages and later monasteries, both known as *palli* in Tamil were places where education was imparted. Consequently, the term *palli* has continued to be used for school to this day. With the establishment of Buddhist monasteries, which also came to be called *palli,* education was provided in these monasteries, too. With the construction of Saiva and Vaishnava temples, Sanskrit learning took place in some of the bigger temples.

Endowments were provided by kings for the maintenance of the temple schools. One of the largest of these schools was at Ennayiram (South Arcot) which received an endowment from Rajendra I. In this school there were 270 junior students, 70 senior students and 14 teachers.

The Thirumukkudal School

An inscription in Thirumukkudal (Chengalpattu) provides one of the best examples of a small Vedic school attached to the Venkatesa Perumal temple there in the eleventh century. This was a school with a hostel. The following are some of the details about this school:

Staff

1 teacher to teach the Rigveda – payment: 60 *kalams* of paddy and 4 *kasu* annually.
1 teacher to teach the Yajurveda – payment same as above.

1 *Bhatta* to expound the *Vyakarana* and the *Rupavatara* – 120 *kalams* of paddy and 10 *kasu* annually.

The hostel attached to the school provided meals for 60 persons daily. This included 40 students in the following categories:

10 Brahmin students studying the Rigveda;10 Brahmin students studying the Yajurveda; 20 Brahmin students studying the *Vyakarana* and the *Rupavatara.* Among the others were 10 Mahapancharatras, 3 Shiva-Brahmanas and 6 Vaikhanasas. Provision was also made for a washerman to wash clothes for the teachers and students.

Meals:

The meals provided to the students consisted of rice and payaru with four curries: ilai-kari (leaf curry), milaku-kari (spicy curry with pepper), pulukku-kari and pulitta- kari. Butter milk was also provided with the meals. The habit of chewing betel after meals seems to have been widely accepted at that time. Provision was, therefore, made to give them betel and arecanut. Three cooks and two maids were employed to prepare the meals.

Provision was also made for the supply of oil for oil-baths on every Saturday, for burning a lamp throughout the night and for repairs and maintenance.

A Teaching Endowment

Temples as well as village assemblies *(sabha)* paid attention to the development of education. Often they were assisted by private endowments. The village assembly of Uttaramerur (whose records on stone are available for more than five centuries) made endowments for teaching grammar, language and other subjects. An example of a teaching endowment *(bhattavritti)* made by a lady is seen in a record at Uttaramerur. It was placed under the supervision of her brother's family and the village assembly. Details of the qualifications for sharing the endowment are given. The teachers who were selected had to reside for three years in a residence provided under the endowment. Pupils were selected after a preliminary examination *(pariksha)*.

Ruins of a hospital in Polonnaruva, Sri Lanka (12th century). Similar hospitals probably existed in Tamil Nadu at that time. Note the stone trough for immersing a patient in herbal water

Section 5 *Tamil Nadu Under One Rule*

4   Local Assemblies: Ur and Sabha

One of the remarkable features of government and administration in ancient Tamil Nadu is the interesting system of local government through the institutions of Ur, Sabha and Nagaram. These local assemblies played an important role in ensuring the continuity and stability of village life.

As early as the beginning of the Common Era, some villages in Tamil Nadu had some sort of a local assembly called *manram* and *potiyil* that looked after the general interest of the village folk. With the cultural and social developments that took place in the later centuries, a more organized local assembly called the Ūr came into being. With the creation of Brahmin settlements as a result of royal grants of villages, a new type of rural settlement called *brahmadeya* or *chaturvedimangalam* also came into existence throughout Tamil Nadu. These had their own assembly called the Sabha or Mahasabha. In the towns established by mercantile communities, another local government institution called the Nagaram emerged. These assemblies had the responsibility for local welfare.

Local groups (gana)

Many stone inscriptions record the activities of these assemblies. These help us to understand the functioning of these institutions. We also get to know about other local groups that assisted these bodies. These were groups that were organized for different purposes. Some were of a religious nature like the Mulaparudaiyar. Some were managers of single shrines in the village, like the Kumāraganam, Krishnaganam, Kāliganam and Viraganam. There were also economic groups like the Valanjiyar and

Manigramam. Others were professional groups *(kalanai)* of carpenters, goldsmiths, and other similar specialised workers.

Uttaramerur Sabha

A local assembly for which we have a considerable number of records spread over nearly five centuries is the Uttaramerur Sabha (Chengalpattu District). These date from 782 CE to 1245 CE.

The activities of the Sabha covered a range of subjects. Clearly, agriculture was the primary concern. The Sabha itself owned land and had responsibility to maintain the irrigation facilities. The main tank, the Vairamegha-tadakam, had to be kept in good repair, with the silt removed every month. The affairs of the main temple, the Vaikuntha-perumal temple, and the other temples in the village, came under the supervision and control of the Sabha.

Endowments: An important function of the Sabha was the administration of a wide variety of endowments to the temples, ranging from those for the daily supply of flowers to those for the teaching of the Vedas and grammar. There were endowments for the recitation of the *Thiruvaymoli* (Vaishnava hymns) and the conduct of festivals.

Committees: To facilitate the conduct of its affairs, the Sabha elected various committees called *vaariyam,* such as the Eri-vaariyam (Tank Committee) and the Thodda-vaariyam (Garden Committee).

Election: The village was divided into thirty wards *(kudumpu)* and each nominated a member (who satisfied the strict qualifications). The names were written on palm-leaves, put into a pot *(kuda-olai),* and a specified number of leaves were picked out by a little boy to form a committee.

Devaradiyar – Temple Dancers

From the sixth century, as many stone temples were built in Tamil Nadu, growing in size in each century, the temple came to occupy a central position in the social, economic and cultural life of the people. Among the arts it helped to develop were dance and music. These arts grew into the Bharathanatyam and Karnataka Sangeetham for which Tamil Nadu is famous today.

Those who helped to develop and preserve the distinctive art of the Bharathanatyam through many centuries of political changes were the humble temple dancers known as the Devaradiyar (Devadasis). Dance, like the singing of devotional hymns, was a form of worship. The Devaradiyal (= Slave of God) dedicated her life to provide this form of worship to the deity of the temple to which she was attached. Every major temple had its dancing girls and their dance masters and drummers.

In the eleventh century, the Rajarajeshvara (Big Temple) at Thanjavur had as many as 400 dancing girls who came from different parts of Tamil Nadu. Each was provided with a separate house and endowments were made for their maintenance. The names and the house numbers of each of the girls assigned to the temple by Rajaraja are inscribed on the temple walls. In the temple, there are sculptured panels depicting the different dance poses (karana) as given in the dance text Natyasastra.

Section 5 *Tamil Nadu Under One Rule*

5   Medical Care – The Veeracholan Hospital

Ayurvedic and other local systems of medicine were practised in Tamil Nadu and some of the well known Sanskrit Ayurvedic texts were taught in certain schools attached to temples. Interesting information about a hospital attached to the Venkatesa Perumal temple at Thirumukkudal is found in an inscription there.

The hospital was named Veeracholan Hospital. The term used for patients was *atular*. The hospital had fifteen beds for patients. The consulting physician was a Brahmin named Savarnan Kodandaraman Asvaththama Bhattar of Alappakkam. The following were the other employees: one person to perform surgical operations; two attendants to collect herbs and fuel for the preparation of drugs; two female nurses to prepare and administer the drugs; and, one barber. A washerman was also employed to wash the clothes of the patients. A full list of the drugs stored in the hospital is given in the inscription. Provision was also made for a lamp to burn throughout the night in the hospital.

Medical Education

After the so-called Sangam poems, Tamil literature is largely religious and devotional. As a result, they are not of great use as sources of history. Inscriptions on stone, mainly in temples, are the most valuable written records we have for the reconstruction of history. While remarkable developments were taking place in the society and economy of Tamil Nadu, unfortunately not much information is available about these in the inscriptions. Medicine, for instance, was studied and practised but there is hardly any information about it in the inscriptions. There is one rare Tamil record dated 1121 CE which has some incidental information about medical education, teachers of medicine and medical students. Ayurvedic medicine was taught and practised in Tamil Nadu. This record gives some information about a medical school attached to a temple at Thiruvaduthurai. At this school two well-known Ayurvedic texts were taught. These were Vagbhata's *Ashtangahrdaya* and the foundational text on Ayurveda, the *Carakasamhita.* Besides the teachers, there was also a *Vaidya* (physician). They were provided with houses near the school (attached to a temple) and given land grants. Meals were supplied for the students in a nearby *matha.*

Section 5 *Tamil Nadu Under One Rule*

6   Irrigation Tanks and Hydraulic Engineering

The magnificent temples in the ancient capital cities of Kanchi, Madurai, Thanjavur and other places, the beautiful bronze images as well as stone sculptures and carvings found in these temples and the thousands of irrigation tanks supplying water for cultivation are among the great achievements of the ancients in Tamil Nadu. Of these, the achievements relating to the construction of irrigation tanks and hydraulic engineering belong to a forgotten chapter of the history of Tamil Nadu.

Rice Farming

As humans began to settle down and live in villages, they domesticated certain plants and animals. They selected certain plants that produced a large amount of nutritious grains and farmed them instead of looking for them in the wild. Among these grains were wheat, barley and rice. More than 8,000 years ago, the Yangzi valley in China was one of the first places where the domestication of rice took place. By 3500 BCE rice farming spread to southern China. From there it spread to Southeast Asia. By 2300 BCE rice farming spread to Thailand.

In the Early Iron Age, that is about 3,000 years ago, rice farming spread to south India and Sri Lanka. Soon rice became the staple diet of the people of this region. Rice farming, along with cattle-keeping, brought about major changes in the hunter-gatherer lifestyle of the people. But for rice cultivation to be successful plenty of water was needed. From the beginning, therefore, village chiefs paid much attention to the supply of water to the villagers. The result was the construction of village tanks.

Veeranam Eri – The Largest Human-made Reservoir in the Ancient World

How many of you have heard of the Veeranam Eri? Perhaps you may have heard that it is the main source of water supply to the City of Chennai. But did you know that it is one of the greatest achievements of the hydraulic engineers of ancient Tamil Nadu? The irrigation engineering technology developed by the ancients for over a thousand years reached its peak in the eleventh century when the Veeranam Eri was built near Jayankonda-cholapuram.

"…it must be remembered that the Cauvery valley had the largest reservoir in the world for nearly a millennium, the Viranam-kulam, near Jayamkonda-cholapuram…, built by the Cholas, a command of 22,000 acres." Sir Joseph Needham (Cambridge scholar and historian of science).

Tanks

When the many small chiefdoms grew into kingdoms, one of the main ideals of the rulers was to ensure an adequate supply of water for rice cultivation through the construction of irrigation tanks and dams. There are legends about the rulers who earned the admiration of the people in fulfilling this duty. Karikal Cholan of the early centuries CE is a hero of some of these legends. A poet of his time praises him for constructing tanks and increasing the fertility of the land.

Since the construction of tanks was considered as an important achievement of a ruler, the chronicles in Sri Lanka have listed the tanks and dams built by every ruler at Anuradhapura. Unfortunately, there are no similar chronicles in Tamil Nadu. We see that the rulers in Sri Lanka built bigger and bigger tanks until in the twelfth century they had some of the largest human-made reservoirs in the world. There was a parallel development in Tamil Nadu which was always in close contact with Sri Lanka. We do not get details of the tanks built in the early centuries CE but from the time of the Pallava rulers we get some information about the tanks built in Tamil Nadu.

Pallava tanks

Kulam was the word used in ancient Tamil for a tank or reservoir. It is still the most commonly used word for a tank. In the time of the Pallavas, the words *eri* and *tadaka* are also used for a tank. At this time we also get the names of the tanks. The Raja-tadakam, the Thiraiyan- eri and the Paramesvara-tadakam were among the earliest tanks. Pallava rulers were no doubt paying attention to the construction of tanks and the names of some of the tanks indicate this. The Paramesvara-tadakam was probably built by Paramesvaravarman and the Mahendra-tadakam (near Sholingur) by Mahendravarman I.

Veeranam (Veera narayana) Eri, Cuddalore District -
constructed in the 11th century.
It was the largest human - made reservoir in the world for
nearly a thousand years.

There was also another Pallava tank called Vairamegha-tadakam, in Uttaramerur. The engineering skills developed to construct tanks seem to have been carried overseas by the traders of Tamil Nadu. These traders built a tank in Thailand and named it Avaninaranam, after a title of Pallava Nandivarman III.

Pandya tanks

The construction and the renovation of tanks were not confined to the Pallava territories. The developments in hydraulic engineering were clearly shared by tank-builders in other parts of Tamil Nadu as well as in Sri Lanka. In the Pandya kingdom a high official of King Sri Mara Sri Vallabha (ninth century CE) enlarged some existing *kulams* into bigger reservoirs *(eri)* in many p[aces, including Tenveliyankudi, Maranur, Iruppaikudi, Koluvur, Nenmali, Siruputtur, Sattanur and Malankudi. In the previous century, the Pandya king Nedumaran devoted his attention to building tanks. In the same century, another Pandya ruler named Chenthan Arikesari excavated a canal *(kaal)* from the Vaigai River.

Advances were made in building long canals and better sluices as well as in the construction of anicuts or dams across rivers. In the time of the Cholas large reservoirs were built and this helped to increase the prosperity of the state. All these developments culminated in the construction of the largest human-made reservoir in the world, the Veeranam-kulam, near Jayankonda –cholapuram, with a capacity of 22,000 acres of water.

Longest Stone Inscription in the World

The Venkatesa Perumal Temple in Thirumukkudal (Chengalpattu District) has the longest stone inscription in the world. Inscribed on the wall of the temple, the inscription is 55 feet (16.76 metres) long and covers an area of nearly 510 sq. feet (nearly 50 sq. metres). It is dated in the sixth regnal year of Virarajendra Chola (= 1069 CE). This ancient record provides information about the wars of Virarajendra, arrangements made for elaborate rituals in the temple and, more importantly, about a Vedic school and a hospital attached to the temple about a thousand years ago.

Section 5 *Tamil Nadu Under One Rule*

7   Foreign Trade – Mercantile Communities

After the decline of Greco-Roman trade in the early centuries CE, the traders of Tamil Nadu looked towards the east. As early as the second and third centuries Indian traders were visiting ports in Thailand and Vietnam. Among them were traders from the Pallava kingdom. They established places of worship in some of the ports and helped to spread Buddhism and the worship of Shiva and Vishnu in these lands. Sanskrit and Tamil inscriptions have been found among the ruins of some of these ancient places of worship.

The growth of mercantile communities is one of the notable developments in the overseas trade of south India from about the sixth century. The ports of Mamallapuram and Nagapattinam on the east coast were linked by a network of trade routes across the Bay of Bengal with ports in Sri Lanka, the port of Takua-pa on the west coast of Thailand and the port of OcEo in southern Vietnam.

One of the earliest mercantile communities trading in Southeast Asia was the Manigramam. This group was active in the west coast port of Kollam and in Takua-pa. The most prominent of these communities was the Ainnuurruvar, sometimes also known as the Nanadesi.

Another community was the Anjuvannam which was of West Asian origin and possibly included Muslim as well as Jewish merchants. These communities dominated the trade with Southeast Asia and some of them sailed even to ports in China.

Muslim traders

In the eleventh century, Arab dominance in the Indian Ocean trade gradually increased. South Indian trading communities continued to have a substantial share of the trade with Southeast Asia. But the south Indian traders were now increasingly Muslim by religion. They came mainly from the Kerala ports of Kollam and Kodungallur and the Tamil Nadu ports of Kayalpattinam, Keelakkarai and Nagapattinam. Slowly the overseas trade of Tamil Nadu and Kerala passed into the traders who were mainly Tamil-speaking Muslims. Through their trade with the Malay kingdoms of Southeast Asia, they were to make a significant contribution towards the spread of Islam in the Malay kingdoms, just as the south Indian traders of the earlier centuries helped to spread, Shaivism, Vaishnavism and Buddhism in Southeast Asia.

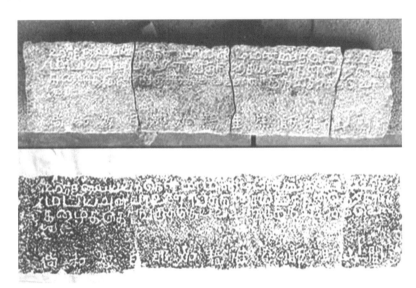

A Tamil inscription in an ancient port in China providing evidence of the activities of merchants from Tamil Nadu in Chinese ports in the time of the Chola rulers.

Section 5 *Tamil Nadu Under One Rule*

8   Coming of Islam

Traders from West Asia were always present in the ports of Tamil Nadu, especially on the west coast, from the centuries before the Common Era. Jewish, Persian and Syrian traders had their settlements in some of these ports. With the birth of Islam in the seventh century, Arab trade increased and more Arab traders settled in the Tamil Nadu ports, married local women and had Tamil-speaking families. Thus began the growth of a community of Muslim Tamils in the ports and market towns of Tamil Nadu, which also extended to the ports of Sri Lanka as well. Some of the earliest Muslim tombs and mosques were built in places like Kollam, Kayalpattinam and Thiruchirapalli.

One of the most interesting documents giving evidence about the early Muslims in the south is the inscription on the Kollam (Quilon) Syrian Copper Plates. These plates were issued by the Kollam ruler Ayyan Adikal to Christian and Muslim merchants, in the ninth century CE.

Through the Muslim traders, Islam spread to the ports of Keelakkarai, Kayalpattinam and Nagapattinam and soon the Muslim Tamils acquired the general name of Sonakar. There were Sonakar merchants in Thanjavur in the time of Rajaraja I. But there were different groups among them, such as the Marakkayar and the Mappila. The overseas trade of Kerala and Tamil Nadu soon came to be dominated by these Muslims and remained so until the arrival of the Europeans. In addition, the very profitable pearl fishery in the sea between Tamil Nadu and Sri Lanka came under their control. Muslim Tamil divers were used for this fishery.

Kollam ruler Ayyan Adikal issued these copper plates to Christian and Muslim merchants including those in the mercantile communities called the Anjuvannam and Manigramam 9th century CE.

Section 5 *Tamil Nadu Under One Rule*

9   The Arts and Literature

Very little is known about the art and architecture of Tamil Nadu for the period before the fifth century. What is known is only through the early Tamil poems. There were temples but they were built of perishable material, mainly wood, and nothing of these temples has survived. There is some information about painting and sculpture. It is about dancing, drama and music that we get much information, especially in the Tamil epics.

The early Pallava rulers introduced stone architecture and sculpture that were already flourishing in Andhra. The first rock-cut cave temples were excavated in the time of Mahendravarman I. The earliest example we have is the cave temple dedicated to Brahma, Vishnu and Shiva at Mandagappattu (South Arcot District). From the cave temples, the move was made to construct temples out of single rocks. These are known as monolithic (= one stone) temples. The best examples are in the ancient Pallava port of Mamallapuram. There are ten of them. Five are in a group popularly known as the Pancha Paandava Rathas.

The change-over from single rock temples to structural or stone brick temples can also be seen in Mamallapuram. This took place in the eighth century. The earliest example of these structural temples is the Shore Temple. It is an excellent work of art and has been standing there out on the shore, exposed to the elements, for more than 1,200 years.

Then came the large Pallava structural temples, of which the Kailasanatha temple and the Vaikunthaperumal temple are magnificent examples.

The Chola rulers continued the traditions of the Pallava builders. A large number of stone temples were built by them throughout their kingdom. With the growth in wealth of the kingdom, the Cholas began to build enormous temples in the eleventh century. Two of these stand out as magnificent examples of these Chola temples. They are the Rajarajesvara Temple built by Rajaraja I at Thanjavur and the equally big temple built by Rajendra I at Gangaikonda-cholapuram. These may be said to mark the peak of the achievements of Chola architecture.

Literature

After the decline of Buddhism and Jainism Tamil literature came to be dominated by Saiva and Vaishnava poets. From about the sixth to about the tenth century Tamil literature was mainly devotional religious. The hymns of the Nayanars and the Alvars as well as those of Manikkavacakar stand out as some of the best products of the Tamil poets in this period.

Sittannavasal : Cave painting in a Rock-cut Jaina monastry 6th - 9th century, Pudukottai

The period of the great Chola emperors was a golden age of Tamil literature. The most prominent poet of this period was

107

Kamban whose *Ramavatharam* is considered to be the greatest epic in Tamil. Kamban is generally held as the greatest of all Tamil poets.

Chola bronze : Nataraja, The Nataraja bronzes of the 11th and 12th centuries have been acclaimed as some of the best examples of the metal sculptures of Tamil Nadu. The French sculptor Auguste Rodin wrote in 1921 that Nataraja has "what many people cannot see – the unknown depths, the core of life. There is grace in elegance, but beyond grace there is perfection."

Gangaikonda - Cholapuram : Sarasvati, 11th century

Section 5 *Tamil Nadu Under One Rule*

10   Missions to China: 1015, 1033 and 1077 CE

Tamil Nadu had contacts with China from the early centuries of the Common Era. Traders from Tamil Nadu began to visit the ports of the ancient kingdoms in Thailand, Malaysia, Cambodia and Vietnam as early as the second and third centuries CE. Possibly some of them went farther to the ports of southern China. Along with the traders went Brahmin priests and Buddhist monks. But embassies from the royal courts went only much later.

There are no records of any of these contacts on the Tamil Nadu side. The Chinese, however, have maintained records of important missions sent from Tamil Nadu. As the trade with the Southeast Asian kingdoms and China assumed greater importance in the eleventh century, the Chola emperors seem to have paid special attention to maintaining good relations with the Chinese emperor.

Rajaraja's embassy

At the beginning of the eleventh century, the Chinese emperor was keen on promoting the trade with foreign lands. Soon there were missions arriving from some of the kingdoms of Southeast Asia. In 1015, a mission arrived from the Chola court. The Chinese records state that the king of the Chola country at that time was Rajaraja. The day this embassy arrived at the Chinese court happened to be the Emperor's birthday. The men from the Chola court watched the celebrations. They gave the emperor pearls and other valuables.

Rajendra's embassy

The overseas campaigns of Rajaraja I seem to have had the aim of controlling the trade with Southeast Asia and China. His son, Rajendra I, continued the same policy and went a step further by attacking the main ports of the Southeast Asian kingdoms. To ensure the continuation of the profitable trade with China, he sent an embassy to the Chinese court. This arrived in the Chinese capital in 1033 CE. Apart from giving the name of the Chola emperor who sent the mission, the Chinese records do not give further details.

Tamil inscription from Quanzhou - 13th century

A Letter from Rajaraja Chola to Zhao Heng - Emperor of China

Early in the eleventh century, the Chola rulers were anxious to promote the overseas trade of their empire and to provide support and protection to their traders. It was a time of intense trade rivalry in the Indian Ocean among the Arabs, the Malays of Southeast Asia (Sri Vijaya and Javanese kingdoms) and the Cholas. They were all eager to trade with China. Consequently, they all sent embassies to the Chinese emperor with expensive gifts. Towards the end of his reign Rajaraja I sent the first Chola embassy to China. It was a large embassy with fifty-two persons. It had a stopover in Sri Vijaya for several months and reached China in 1015 CE. By that time Rajaraja had died and was succeeded by Rajendra I.

Zhao Heng

The Chinese royal court has carefully preserved records of missions sent to China. In the Chinese book *Wen Xiang Tong Kao* (Comprehensive Textual Research of Historical Documents), the wood blocks of which are still in the Beijing National Palace Museum, it is stated that Rajaraja sent the following letter to the Emperor of China, who at that time was the Song dynasty ruler Zhao Heng. Part of the letter reads as follows:

"My age, the stretch of the seas that separate us, and the great difficulties on the route to traverse, do not permit me to go, in order to carry myself the tribute that I wish to offer you…[This will therefore be done by] my envoys, to the number of fifty-two, arriving at the foot of your throne. I have ordered them to offer you a robe and a cap decorated with pearls, pearls of different sizes weighing about 21,000 liang, sixty pieces of ivory and sixty pounds of incense."

Rajaraja
(a late sculpture believed to be that of Rajaraja)

Rajaraja would have been fully informed about the importance of the China trade and the might of the Chinese emperor by the leaders of the trading communities. The Chinese for their part, were anxious to promote the trade with foreign merchants. In fact, two years after Rajaraja ascended the throne, that is in 987 CE, which was the first year of the reign of Emperor Zhao Heng, the Chinese sent four missions with gifts to foreign rulers requesting them to send traders more frequently to Chinese ports and assuring them of special facilities. It is not known whether Rajaraja received one of these missions and whether his mission was in response to the Chinese request.

Kulottunga's embassy

Very early in his reign Kulottunga I showed interest in maintaining good relations with the Chinese court. In 1077 the Chinese court received an embassy sent by Kulottunga. We are told that 72 men formed this embassy. They presented the emperor a number of articles, including ivory and cloves. In return, they received 81,800 strings of copper cash. Kulottunga's name also appears to be inscribed in a Chinese inscription of this time.

Elephant worshipping Shivalingam, Museum of Maritime History, Quanzhou

Archaeological remains in the ancient Chinese port of Quanzhou establishes beyond doubt that there was a community of traders from Tamil Nadu living in that port. The Kaiyuan Temple there preserves many of the sculptures from a temple of Shiva. Carvings from a Hindu temple, including a big image of Vishnu are kept in the Quangzhou Maritime Museum. In the thirteenth century, the Tamil traders in Qunagzhou built a Shiva temple, with the permission of the

114

emperor, and named it Thiru-kaanisvaram (presumably after Kublai Khan who was the emperor at that time). The Tamil inscription that gives this information is now kept in the Xiamen University Museum.

Section 5 *Tamil Nadu Under One Rule*

11   The Decline of Chola Power

When Rajendra Chola died in 1044, the Chola empire was still intact. But soon trouble started in the territories outside the Chola kingdom. In the north, there was constant conflict with the Western Chalukyas. There was rebellion in Sri Lanka and opposition was brewing in the Pandya and Kerala territories. But Rajadhiraja, who succeeded Rajendra, and Virarajendra who ruled after him, managed to keep the empire together. With the death of Virarajendra in 1069 Chola power faced challenges at various fronts.

In 1070, a grandson of Rajendra I became the Chola ruler with the name of Kulottunga. He was brought up in the Eastern Chalukya court because his father was an Eastern Chalukya prince. Almost immediately after he became king, Chola rule ended in Sri Lanka. He had to fight many wars with the Western Chalukyas and others to maintain Chola rule in the Telugu territories. The Cholas lost most of these territories and, towards the end of Kulottunga's reign, their power was confined to the Tamil country. However, Kulottunga's reign was a period of prosperity. He is ranked among the great Chola rulers.

After Kulottunga's death in 1122, the Chola rulers faced many revolts in their empire. Of these, the most important was the problem faced in the Pandya territory. Several wars were fought here but the Cholas could not keep the Pandyas loyal to them for long. The Sri Lankan ruler Parakramabahu also entered the fray and sent his armies to help some of the Pandya princes. By the end of the twelfth century Chola power declined and gave way to the rise of the Pandyas. By that time, the Chalukya empire had disappeared. Until the end of the 12th century, Tamil Nadu was free from the invasions and political turmoils that troubled the north Indian kingdoms. All this was to change soon. A new era dawned in the 13th century.

Kerala Separates

From ancient times the territory of the modern Kerala state formed part of what was known as Tamilakam. By the ninth century we see the beginnings of a separate geographical unit called Kerala. The rise of the kingdom of Mahodayapuram (also known as Makkotai) marks the beginning of the separation of Kerala from Tamil Nadu. It also marks the beginning of a new era in the history of Kerala. Its identity, separate from that of the rest of Tamilakam, takes shape from this time. The rulers of Mahodayapuram, known as the Perumals, claimed to be overlords of a separate country called Kerala (Keraladhinatha), a territorial name that definitely comes into use in the ninth century. The Perumals also began to use Old Malayalam in their inscriptions, whereas the earlier rulers in that region had used Tamil. From the ninth century, the rulers of the neighbouring kingdoms of the Cholas, Pandyas and the Sinhalas recognized Kerala as a separate kingdom.

For Further Reading

For those interested in getting more information and explanation:

1. A very readable and interesting book on the origins of humans in Africa and their long journey out of that continent to other parts of the world is *The Incredible Human Journey* by Alice Roberts (London 2009). For those interested in greater scientific details, *The Human Past,* edited by the Cambridge archaeologist Chris Scarre (London 2005) is a valuable reference book.

2. For the Indian background, from the time of the Indus valley civilization to the period of the Mauryan Empire, Romila Thapar's *The Penguin History of Early India* (London 2001) is an excellent book.

3. To get some details about the laborious work done by scholars to unfold the story of India's great emperor Ashoka and to know about the young British scholars who pioneered this task, a very fascinating book is *Ashoka: The Search for India's Lost Emperor* by Charles Allen (London 2012). It is a real labour of love.

4. *A Concise History of South India: Issues and Interpretations,* ed. Noboru Karashima (with contributions from Y. Subbarayalu and other scholars), Oxford University Press, New Delhi 2014. This book deals with recent advances in the study of South India and presents new perspectives on many issues relating to the culture and history of the region.

5. K.A. Nilakanta Sastri, *A History of South India,* with an Introduction by R. Champakalakshmi, Oxford University Press, New Delhi 1999. This has remained for a long time as a brilliant narrative of South Indian history. Though somewhat outdated, it remains a classic work.

6. Charles Allen, *Coromandel: A Personal History of South India,* 2017. This very readable and interesting book deals with aspects of South India's cultural history which the author found fascinating and challenging. It is written for a general readership from the point of view of a secular humanist.

THANKS

My grateful thanks are due to Kumaran, Agnas, Sarvam, Pavithra, Romeshun, Harini, Dharini, Chandra, Aravindan, Priya, Meghana, Maya, Vivek and Mira for their help and encouragement to publish this book.

K. Indrapala

Made in United States
Troutdale, OR
11/13/2024

24733241R00070